SECRET TACTICS

✻

SECRET TACTICS

Lessons from the Great Masters of Martial Arts

KAZUMI TABATA

TUTTLE PUBLISHING
Boston · Rutland,Vermont · Tokyo

First published in 2003 by Tuttle Publishing, an imprint of Periplus Editions (HK) Ltd., with editorial offices at 153 Milk Street, Boston, Massachusetts 02109.

Library of Congress Cataloging-in-Publication Data
Tabata, Kazumi
Secret tactics : lessons from the great masters of martial arts / Kazumi Tabata.
p. cm.
ISBN: 0-8048-3488-1
LCC: 2003106321

Distributed by

North America, Latin America, and Europe
Tuttle Publishing
Distribution Center
Airport Industrial Park
364 North Clarendon, VT 05759-9436
Tel: (802) 773-8930
Fax: (802) 773-6993
Email: info@tuttlepublishing.com

Asia Pacific
Berkeley Books Pte. Ltd.
130 Joo Seng Road
#06-01/03 Olivine Building
Singapore 368357
Tel: (65) 6280-3320
Fax: (65) 6280-6290
Email: inquiries@periplus.com.sg

Japan
Tuttle Publishing
Yaekari Bldg., 3F
5-4-12 Ōsaki, Shinagawa-ku
Tokyo 141-0032
Tel: (03) 5437-0171
Fax: (03) 5437-0755
Email: tuttle-sales@gol.com

First edition
08 07 06 05 04 03   9 8 7 6 5 4 3

Book design by Victor Mingovits

Printed in the United States of America

TABLE OF CONTENTS

RECOMMENDATION

The knowledge inherited from the long history of Asia is compiled in this book as a collection of thoughts. This is an extremely unique book in that it expresses the form and shape of the fighting psyche and spirit through martial arts. I have never before encountered such a finely distilled book. While perusing the book, I felt I could almost touch the core of life. It is an honor for me to encounter this book and I wish to recommend it to as many people as possible. This book also revives the old classics to modernity and is a guidebook to the art of living. I believe it speaks to people from all walks of life and could serve as a good reference. Originator and teacher Kazumi Tabata is one who has been investigating the space and Zen of Karate.

Karate is a way of learning truth. The traditional skill and the truth hidden in the word "Karate" are gleaned from training. When these experiences are analyzed scientifically and psychologically, and researched using perspectives from sports psychology, religion, meditation, breathing techniques, and personal viewpoints, the way of truth is opened. This part certainly is not glossed over in the book. This book is not just about Karate, but presents a unique worldview that surpasses Karate.

Shihan Tabata trained in the Shotokan style in the Karate Club of Waseda University. After graduation, he studied under Hisao Obata (a leading student of Gichin Funakoshi) who was then at Keio Private University and was the first Chief Director of the Japan Karatedo Federation. The study of "do" in "Karatedo" and the approaches and interpretations initiated by Obata are included within this book.

Shihan Tabata was the first instructor dispatched to the U.S. in 1967, before a system for sending instructors overseas had been initiated by the Japan Karate Federation. He has been teaching Karatedo in various countries with a base in Boston. His excellent leadership and instruction, coupled with his broad-minded and cheerful disposition, have led him to mix and integrate well with people and communities in every country. He has been playing an active role as an international goodwill ambassador, in addition to teaching Karatedo.

He was a close friend of the late Dr. Takaichi Mano, the former Chief Director of the Japan Karatedo Federation, and served as an advisor when Dr. Mano took office as the General Secretary of the World Karate Federation.

After he was dispatched to the U.S., Shihan Tabata did not slow down the pace of his own study, but continued the in-depth research of etiquette, Okinawan Kobudo, and Zen, which makes profound his martial arts techniques and spirit.

I hold in high regard the content and passion of this publication. I sincerely hope this book will lead to the development and growth of its readers.

April 2000

Keiichi Hasumi
Vice President and General Secretary,
Japan Karatedo Federation

PREFACE

In today's material culture, the ability to cultivate the mind—an important component of human existence—is said to have been lost. Assuming that this is the case, it is important that we return to the quest for the origin of the mind of vast nature and the soul of the universe.

What is this religious mind encompassing the universe? What is the state of mind that is shaped through training in the martial arts?

The body and consciousness. Confusion and anxiety. The way to attain peace of mind. Happiness in life and its possessors. The exquisite tactics. I freely picked up a pen to write of the world of techniques and mind from my own experience and from those who came before me.

There is no easy way to master the secrets of the world. Continuous training and fervent disciplining of the body unveil hidden knowledge, paving the way for mastering the secret of things. Innately, our mind has exquisite tactics with complete control. Those who are referred to as tacticians of great caliber shed luster by virtue of many years of hard training and effort.

In contrast, those who are innately dexterous tend to have difficulty in sustaining their enthusiasm for training over long years. This disposition derives from the fact that they lose their interest in training once they have learned the basics. When a conceited thought appears, techniques and mind will not further advance. A true tactician thinks of nothing but improving his techniques without conceit.

Therefore, never miss daily training. Always try to improve your technique through trial and error. This will slowly build a foundation for your mind. Then, suddenly, the acquisition of invincible techniques will be achieved. With our mind's eyes open we will be able to hear the chatter of birds, the sound of wind, and the principle of the universe. One will be able to anticipate the intention of one's opponent before he strikes or before he opens his mouth. Attacks will seem as if they approach in slow motion. The highest skill leading to invincibility can be achieved only with a first-rate mind.

I would be delighted if this book could contribute to the success of its readers in any way.

Gasshou!
Kazumi Tabata

BOOK ONE

THE BOOK OF SEVEN MASTERS

"Hear the sound of wind and water."

THE MOST IMPORTANT FACTOR in studying the martial arts is not merely to understand, but to transcend rationale and technique. Mastering both of these concepts is necessary and, like the two wheels of a cart, neither will be useful if one is missing.

In the martial arts, the spiritual aspect is the most important, and our forerunners, who were swordsmen of genius, have left legacies gathered from their personal encounters. Here I have collected works that I feel are most pertinent to the true understanding of the martial arts. These books were written between the fifteenth and sixteenth centuries, a time in Japanese history of warring states and attempts at unification. During this period, the art of war was not merely a sport or spiritual training; this was a time when one's existence depended on one's skill in destroying the enemy. These works, the records of men who lived by the sword in harsh times, contain valuable lessons for us today.

Ki

HEI-HO-KADEN-SHO
Hereditary Manual of the Martial Arts

By Yagyu Tajimanokami Munenori

"Stealing glances at a bird, a dragonfly keeps away from it."

IT IS WELL KNOWN that Zen philosophy underlies Japanese culture. Zen philosophy is more concrete and experiential than abstract and
intellectual. One of the books that can give a glimpse of the original Zen
philosophy is Hei-Ho-Kaden-Sho, the Hereditary Book of
the Martial Arts. Hei-Ho-Kaden-Sho, which we are going to
introduce here, was written by Yagyu Munenori, Lord of Tajima, the most
respected master serving the Tokugawa Shogun family. Munenori was born
near the end of the Sengoku Period, or the Age of the Country at War.
After having survived this period of warfare, Munenori decided to trans-
mit to succeeding generations the theories and techniques of battle that
he had acquired through his great experience. However, his contribution
is not only that he wrote Hei-Ho-Kaden-Sho (abbreviated as
Kadensho), but also that he elevated the martial arts to include the
government of nations as well as the use of sword. For this reason, his
sword was called the "sword for the shogun, for the government, and for
the world."

The main part of Kadensho is devoted to detailed accounts of how
to control the mind during fighting and what kinds of training are necessary for such control of the mind. The book discusses the principles of
battle that Munenori systematized through his lifelong martial training,
and furthermore tries to extend the application of such principles to social
and political life as a whole. Thus, Kadensho, full of lessons relevant
to every aspect of life, is truly said to be the essence of battle, and of life

itself. The book has profound significance even today, when pursuit of humane and spiritual knowledge is fundamental to many.

Born in 1571 as the fifth son of Sekishusai Muneyoshi, Munenori came to serve the second shogun, Tokugawa Hidetada, as a Hei-Ho instructor. He died March 26, 1647 at the age of 76.

We present excerpts from this work.

Hei Ho   Kaden Sho

THE PHILOSOPHY AND SECRETS OF STRATEGY

The ultimate purpose of practicing swordsmanship is to make the art thoroughly a part of oneself. It is necessary to achieve a state in which one is able to use optimum techniques reflexively and unconsciously. One can accomplish this by learning to cope with every possible circumstance. When wielding the sword at the enemy, do not allow your soul to attach itself to the technique. If the soul is attached, the enemy will have the opportunity to strike back and cause you to lose. When the sword is wielded, do not think about whether you have killed your opponent, but rather strike with all your might. Do not allow the enemy to raise his face.

When the outward appearance is spirited, the inner self is calm; when the outward appearance is aggressive, the inner self is defensive; thus, make the state of the inner self the opposite of the outward appearance. Through continuous practice, the outer and inner selves will become one.

No matter how splendid one's technique, if one's soul has attached itself to that technique, then one cannot win. It is important to practice without attaching one's soul to thoughts of striking or thrusting.

A GATE IS THE VESTIBULE TO A HOUSE

The books of Confucius are thought of as a gate to those who devote their mind to learning. What is a gate? A gate is the entrance to a house. Only by going through the gate can one meet the master of the house. Learning, for example, is the gate to truth. Only by going through the gate can you obtain truth. Opening the gate should not be mistaken for having entered the house, for the house lies beyond the gate.

TRAIN YOURSELF THOROUGHLY

Once you have trained yourself well, your body and limbs will move automatically without any conscious effort. Your mind will not be overwhelmed by your physical movements. You will employ techniques unconsciously without having to think. Once you have attained this state of mind, not a single doubt nor hesitation will arise. No opponent, not even the devil, will find an opportunity to attack. Train yourself thoroughly and then forget about it. Throw away your mind.

You will follow the way without being aware of it. This is the mystery of the way.

ALL FALSEHOOD BECOMES TRUTH

A well-devised game plan is basic to strategy. A stratagem should be devised so that your opponent cannot resist it even if he is aware of it.

Trap your opponent. If he falls into your plan, you will defeat him. If you judge your plan to be faulty, devise another immediately. Your opponent will eventually be trapped. This is similar to the idea of *hoben* in Buddhist terminology. Using hoben (a white lie) one pretends to hide one's real intention within. Since hoben fulfills your initial purpose eventually, your deception brings success. In Shintoist terminology this is called *shimpi* (a mystery).

Shimpi raises false security among people. By keeping things mysterious the perpetrator reaps benefits. This is also called *buryaku* (military strategy) in martial arts terminology.

Ryaku (strategy) means falsehood—to be exact, the utilization of falsehood to ensure victory without loss on your side. The application of deceptive techniques demonstrates that the use of trickery can eventually lead to success. The white lie can aid you in reaching your goal.

THE OFFENSIVE AND THE DEFENSIVE

Insofar as you and your opponent are both in an offensive position, the opponent's state of mind does not differ from yours. In the offensive position concentrate your mind on your opponent. The moment you start a match, attack your opponent intensely and use your initiative. When on the defensive guard against your opponent, wait for his move then immediately switch to the offensive.

HOW TO TRAP THE OPPONENT

The relationship between the offensive and the defensive parallels the relationship between the sword and the body. Hold your sword in a defensive position; place your body close to your opponent and maintain an offensive posture; the offensive posture of your body should cause your opponent to make the first attack. You will defeat him if you are prepared for his move.

CONTROL THE RELATIONSHIP
BETWEEN MIND AND BODY

The relationship between the offensive and the defensive also parallels that between mind and body. The mind should be on the cautious defensive; the body should be on the offensive. Without a cautious mind one often becomes reckless. If the mind is on the offensive, defeat must unavoidably result.

SEEING WITHOUT SEEING

It is crucial not to fix your eyes on one place. There is a poem that reads: "Stealing glances at a bird, a dragonfly keeps away from it. The dragonfly moves attentively, stealing glances at its enemy's motion."

In judging your opponent's reaction to the trap you set for him, see him without looking at him; that is, do not fix your eyes on one place. Keep your eyes in motion all the time, and catch glimpses between each movement.

KEEP STRIKING—DO NOT LET YOUR
OPPONENT RAISE HIS HEAD

To avoid being struck is more difficult than to strike. When the opponent strikes, allow enough space between yourself and your opponent so that his sword will not reach your body, then let his stroke follow. If you allow a safe distance, the opponent's unsuccessful stroke will turn into a "dead stroke." Taking advantage of this chance, step forward immediately and defeat the opponent.

Once you deliver the first stroke, never allow the opponent time to recover. Whether or not your first stroke is successful, continue to strike repeatedly, thereby not allowing him to raise his head. In this way, your first stroke can lead to victory. Never imagine that you are safe after you deal a blow to the opponent. If you stop your attack, it will give him a good chance to recover and may very likely result in your defeat. This happens because your mind dwells upon the first stroke you have delivered and thus becomes inattentive to the opponent's counterattack. Such an inattentive mind will make your first successful blow lose its value.

DEFEAT THE OPPONENT
BY MANIPULATING RHYTHM

If the opponent's stroke has a slow rhythm, counter with a faster rhythm. If his stroke has a fast rhythm, counter with a slower rhythm. Deliver the kind of strokes that do not harmonize with the opponent's strokes.

If the opponent finds the rhythm of your stroke agreeable, he will feel it easier to deliver his strokes. A skillful singer of *utai* (the Noh songs) does not sing with fixed tones; he constantly and delicately changes his tones, making it difficult for an unskillful drummer to beat his drum in harmony with the song.

Just as a poor drummer would disturb a skillful utai singer and a poor utai singer would disturb a skillful drummer, so do unrhythmical strokes disturb your opponent. The technique of utilizing such combinations is called "*obyoshi kobyoshi, kobyoshi obyoshi*" (slow beat fast beat, fast beat slow beat).

A good bird catcher holds his net in such a way that a bird can see it well. While shaking the pole he brings it closer to the bird and eventually catches it. The bird is so absorbed by the rhythm of the shaking pole that somehow it is unable to fly away and is captured in spite of its fluttering and its intention to leave.

Do not harmonize with the rhythm of your opponent's strokes. If the opponent gets out of rhythm, he will even fail to jump over a small gutter. Study such a state of mind carefully.

GRASP THE TOTALITY OF
YOUR OPPONENT'S MOVEMENTS

You could not act in the Noh (a classical dance) or sing utai without understanding the totality of the music. The case is the same with martial arts. It is important to judge correctly your opponent's strokes and movements. Once you grasp the flow of the opponent's motion, you can defeat him with greater ease.

PREPARE FOR THE OFFENSIVE OPPONENT

Strategy is fundamental in martial arts. The important thing is for you to take advantage of the opponent's initial move for which you should design various strategies.

Before the match begins, brace yourself, and prepare yourself for the offensive opponent. For this purpose, you should strengthen your mind for the defense. If you face the opponent without being prepared for his offensive attitude, his surprise attack may turn out so successfully that you will be unable to bring your training into full play.

BE CALM OUTSIDE, BE RIGOROUS INSIDE

"Hear the sound of wind and water" means that you should be calm outside but keep your mind alert and prepared. The wind has no sound, but it makes sound when striking things. When the wind blows high it remains quiet, but when it comes down and strikes trees and bamboo, it moves busily and makes sound.

Likewise, falling water has no sound. It is noisy only when it strikes objects.

"Hear the sound of wind and water" is a metaphorical expression for having an exterior appearance of quiet and an internally active mind. Your body and arms and legs should not appear busy.

Meanwhile, you must be careful to balance the relationship between the offensive and the defensive, between exterior and interior. Have a state of mind that will enable you to switch from yin (negative) to yang (positive), and from yang to yin. Action is yang; stillness is yin.

When your inside turns to yang, or action, keep your outside in the state of yin, or stillness. When your interior remains yin, keep your exterior yang. This is the case in strategy. This corresponds with the nature of things. When your action is on the offensive, you should keep your mind still and not let it go along with your exterior. By keeping your mind still, you can better control your action.

If your exterior and interior are both active, neither will be under control. Alternate the offensive and the defensive, action and stillness. Just as a duck appears calm on water while keeping its webbed feet busy underwater, similarly, a well-trained strategist will seem calm outwardly, while keeping his interior active. It is the purpose of strategy to reach a state of mind that can fully control the alternation of the offensive and the defensive, action and stillness.

About the saying "Hear the sound of wind and water" Yagyu Jubei Mitsuyoshi, the oldest son of Yagyu Munenori, teaches that even during a match your mind should not be so preoccupied with your opponent that you cannot hear the sound of wind and water.

A FIXED MIND IS DISEASED

It is a disease to be possessed by ideas of victory or of technique. It is also a disease to be possessed by the idea of showing the results of your training. It is a disease to be determined to attack first or, conversely, to wait for the opponent's move. It is a disease even to be possessed by the idea of removing all such diseases.

The disease is a state of mind that is rigid and fixed, in whatever situation. All such diseases stem from your state of mind. It is important to control the mind.

REMOVE THOUGHTS BY MEANS OF THOUGHTS

A saying, literally translated, states, "One has thoughts, and yet no thoughts; one has persistence, and yet no persistence." This means that fixing one's thoughts on expelling a disease is just another disease, or that even being possessed by the thought that your mind is unsound is such a fixed thought, and therefore a disease.

A state of mind having no thoughts is called "munen" or freedom from all thoughts. You can reach munen by removing thoughts through means of other thoughts.

When one thought removes the other, the disease of the mind, both the thoughts of removing and the removed thought will vanish together; just as two wedges come off when one wedge is used to detach the other.

A fixed wedge will be loosened if another wedge is driven in beside it. The second wedge will also be loosened, and nothing will remain.

Similarly, if a thought—the disease of the mind—goes away, the thought that removes the first thought will also go away. This is what is meant by "One has thoughts, and yet no thoughts."

TRAIN YOUR MIND SO AS
NOT TO BE BOTHERED BY A DISEASE

A higher level of mental training is to remove a disease by giving up any efforts to remove it. It has already been observed that it is a disease to be possessed by the idea of expelling a disease. Then, why can't we expel a disease by leaving ourselves in a state of disease? After all, trying to remove a disease means keeping it in your mind. A disease is a fixed mind.

After completing a higher level of training, you will naturally free yourself from fixed thoughts without trying to do so. In Buddhism, a fixed mind is the first thing to be avoided. A Buddhist free from a fixed mind would not be corrupted even in a tumultuous crowd. He would always be free and carried away by nothing.

Even if you have a profound knowledge of techniques in some field, you cannot be called "master" of the techniques unless your knowledge is flexible. This is true in any field of endeavor.

Unpolished stones gather dust easily, but completely polished stones remain shining even in mud. Polish your mind so that you can leave it free and undisturbed by disease.

ACT WITH YOUR ORDINARY STATE OF MIND

A Buddhist priest asked a higher priest, "What is the way?" The higher priest answered, "Your ordinary state of mind is the way." This expresses the state of mind in which you can remove a disease by leaving yourself diseased, that is, by using your natural state of mind.

The same thing is applicable to many other things. In archery, if you are absorbed by the thought of hitting the mark you will have difficulty even in aiming. In sword matches, if you are absorbed by the thought of delivering strokes, you will have difficulty in controlling your sword. In calligraphy, if you are possessed by the idea of drawing, your brush will not move freely. Or in playing the koto, if you are possessed by the thought of playing, you will get out of tune.

What should you do? Stop thinking that you are going to hit at the mark. You can take better aim in your ordinary state of mind. This refers to your mind when you are doing nothing in particular.

Strike with your sword, ride a horse, draw letters, or play the koto with as natural a state of mind as you would have if you were doing none of these things. With such a mind everything will become easier.

In whatever field, the true way is other than being possessed by the idea that there is a prescribed way to do it. A master of the way is someone whose mind is not stuck; such a person can achieve anything easily. A mirror clearly reflects appearance simply because the mirror itself has no appearance.

A master of the way can deal with any given situation because his mind is like a clear mirror; it is totally free from all thought. This is your ordinary state of mind, and only he who accomplishes everything with such a mind deserves the title of master.

CARRY THE MIND THAT WOULD,
WHEN RELEASED, NOT STAY IN ONE PLACE

Abbot Chuho, a Mongolian high priest, taught his disciples to have a released mind, or "*hoshin no kokoro.*" His teaching has two levels of meaning. At the lower level, it means, "Train yourself so that you can withdraw your released mind before it stays affixed." When you deliver a stroke, withdraw your sword swiftly so that your mind will not stay where the sword goes.

In the higher level, it means, "Release your mind and let it go freely wherever it wants as long as it does not stay in one place." The mind tied with a rope cannot be free.

Free motion of your body and limbs is possible only with such a released mind. Leave your dogs and cats free. Nothing would be more awful than chained-up dogs and cats.

A WELL-DISCIPLINED MIND

Confucians consider the concept of *kei* (veneration) as the highest possible state of mind. Leading their lives in this state of mind, they are like chained cats; they keep their mind captive.

It is true that Buddhism too has the concept of kei; Buddhist scriptures teach *isshin furan,* or wholeheartedness, which is the counterpart of the Confucian concept of kei. This is the state of mind in which you concentrate on one thing and thereby are disturbed by nothing else.

It is said that kei is the true Buddhist's attitude. That is, a Buddhist devotes his wholehearted respect to the statue of Buddha. This is what kei means. However, it should not be forgotten that this is a means to keep your mind peaceful; a well-disciplined mind does not need this means.

Take the proper posture, press your palms together, repeat "Fudomyo-o," aloud, and keep the image of fudomyo-o in your mind. Then body, mouth, and mind will be unified into one, and you will find your mind quiet and peaceful. Such a state is called *sanmitsu byodo*, or equality of the three secrets; it is in harmony with the concept of kei.

This state of mind is like that of prayer. Once you stop pressing your palms together and repeating Buddha's name, the image of Buddha will disappear from your mind. Your mind will return to a state of unrest. Such a condition is lacking in mental discipline.

Someone who can truly control his mind need not purify his body, mouth, or mind in particular. Such a person will not be corrupted even in a tumultuous crowd and will not be affected by changes in his environment: it is just like the moon, which itself remains the same while the image of the moon on water changes as the tide surges. Such is the state of those who reach the truth of Buddhism.

THE TECHNIQUE OF MUTO (NO SWORD)

Muto is a technique of avoiding the strokes delivered by your opponent, especially when you are not armed. It is not necessarily a technique of taking away your opponent's sword, for trying to take away your opponent's sword is not admirable in itself. Indeed, letting your opponent hold his sword, especially if he is absorbed in it, is one variation of the technique of muto.

The opponent who is absorbed in guarding his sword cannot pay attention to attacking you. If you are not struck, it is your victory. The point of the technique is not to take away your opponent's sword, but to avoid being struck, or more precisely, to use effectively whatever is at your disposal to avoid being struck.

That you can take away your opponent's sword for your own use indicates symbolically that you are trained well enough to use anything for a weapon. Even a tiny fan might be used to defeat an armed opponent. Such is the secret of muto.

Suppose you were walking unarmed, perhaps just with a bamboo cane. Then, if you were attacked, you should ward off your opponent's sword with the bamboo cane and take away his sword. Even if you fail to take his sword, you do not allow him to strike you. This is already your victory. This is the meaning of the technique of muto.

MA'AI (DISTANCE): THE CORE OF MUTO

The true aim of muto is to train your sense of mai'ai, or space, to sharpen your judgment of how far away from your opponent you should take your stance in order to avoid his thrust.

As long as you allow enough space between yourself and your opponent, you need not be afraid of his thrust. The sooner you judge whether you are within the reach of your opponent's thrust, the sooner you can consider the next step to take.

The technique of muto cannot be practiced unless you are within the reach of the opponent's thrust. That is to say, you can only take away the sword from the opponent by exposing yourself to his thrust.

DUCK BENEATH THE SHAFT
OF YOUR OPPONENT'S SWORD

Muto is also the technique of fighting your armed opponent with bare hands. A sword, of course, is longer than your hand. This means that you cannot practice the technique without placing yourself so close to your opponent that you could be struck.

Duck under the shaft of your opponent's sword and take away his sword while he is swinging it over your head. This will vary according to the situation, but the plain fact is that you cannot remove the opponent's sword without drawing close to him.

KI (JUDGMENT AND WILL) SUBSISTS INWARD,
AND YU (ACTION) SUBSISTS OUTWARD

Everything has its substance and action. For example, shooting an arrow and hitting the target are the actions of a bow. A lamp is substance, and light is its action. Water is substance, and wetness is its action. A plum blossom is substance, and its fragrance and color are its action. A sword is substance, and delivering a stroke is action. Will is substance, and its effect on the outside is action. Because a plum exists (substance), the plum trees blossom, exhibit colors, and emit fragrance.

Similarly, because your will exists within you, your actions come outwardly. Hence you stroke, thrust, set a trap, take the offensive and defensive position, and so forth. The outward subsistent will is called *sayo*, or action.

Only a great will results in a large action. A well-disciplined Zen master has such a free mind that whatever he says and does never deviates from the way—the nature of things.

A WHOLE BODY DISPLAYS ITS ABILITY

Jintu Shinpen (godly power or transformation) does not mean that gods descend from the heavens and perform miracles. It refers to someone capable of totally free action.

Daiyu, or great action, can be described through actions such as holding a sword, jumping up and down, taking away the opponent's sword, kicking down, and so on, without being bothered by conventional patterns of practice. Even if you neglect to cultivate your will regularly, daiyu will emerge when necessary. For example, when you sit in a room you should observe the ceiling and make sure there's nothing to fall upon you.

When you take a seat near a door or screen, keep your mind alert; they may open or fall down on you at any time. Be alert when you pass a gate. Ki, or will and judgment, should always be alert in this way.

If you hold such an attentive ki, you can act swiftly at the time of an unexpected event. Daiyu is such a swift action.

If ki is still immature, sayo will not come out. By continuing to train your mind, you will develop a mature ki that will enable daiyu to emerge. If ki is rigidly fixed, sayo will not work. When ki is reaching the ultimate stage, it spreads throughout the body; therefore daiyu will also act throughout every part of the body.

If you rely solely on the results of practice, you may not be able to raise your hand when you face someone who has *daiki daiyu*. People speak about *mizume*, the defeat of sight.

Mizume is a defeated state in which the gaze of someone with *daiki* absorbs you so deeply that you forget about your sword. Even if this were momentary, it could result in your defeat; as in the case of a rat watched by a cat that missed its step and fell off a beam. A person of daiki is to a person of no daiki what the cat is to the rat.

ACTION FREE FROM CONVENTIONS

Zen Buddhism says, "Where daiyu reveals itself fully, there is no such thing as following rules and conventions." Someone who achieves daiki daiyu does not adhere to the established patterns of practice and rules.

Some rules and conventions are necessary in any field of life. But someone who reaches perfection can forget about such rules and conventions. He can act completely freely. A man of daiki is such a person.

Ki is a state of mind that is prepared for anything. If ki is rigid, it will restrain the mind and hence deprive it of freedom. Free action is possible only when ki is completed and spreads throughout the body. Such free action is called dai-yu.

THE TRAINING OF HIDING YOUR MIND

There is a saying: "The mind changes as its environment changes. Such a change is subtle—so subtle that you cannot perceive it." This is extremely important for martial arts as well as for Zen training. For someone not familiar with Zen, it may be hard to understand.

To use the terminology of the martial arts, "the environment" is the opponent's various movements. Thus, the first sentence states that your mental attitude changes as your opponent's movement changes. In other words, when the opponent swings his sword over his head, your mind turns toward the direction of his sword. When he swings his sword to the right, your mind directs itself that way; when he moves the sword to the left, your mind works that way, and so on.

The meaning of "you cannot perceive the change" is important for the martial arts. It means that since the mind stays nowhere and leaves nothing behind, it cannot be perceived for certain. You must bear in mind what is implied here. A resting mind will give way to the conventional techniques of martial arts. The mind that stops changing and becomes rigid will result in disaster. While mind, with no color and no shape, is imperceptible to the eyes, it is still recognizable if it is fixed and strays over something. Just as white silk turns red in color when it is stained with red dyes, similarly the human mind becomes visible if it is stained with an emotion or thought, for example, a girl's secret affection for a boy will show up sooner or later. It is like the saying, "If you have something on your mind, your face reveals it."

MARTIAL ARTS—ZEN

There are many things in common between martial arts and Buddhism, particularly Zen. Most importantly, they share repugnance toward an affixed mind or a fixed point of view. In answer to a poem that the Buddhist Saigyo wrote at a brothel in Eguchi, a woman read the following poem:

> *For someone like yourself, joining the priesthood, this world must be as temporary as this house is. Just hope you would not leave your mind here.*

The second line conveys something very important for students of the martial arts. Whatever *gokui*, or mastered secret, you learn, you will be defeated if you stick to fixed techniques. It is always more important to train yourself so that you can keep your mind from stopping at one place.

YOUR ORDINARY STATE OF MIND IS EVERYTHING

A master of strategy is someone who has mastered all the techniques and then has given them up altogether. He always acts with his natural state of mind. This must be the case in any other field of life as well. If a strategist is possessed by the thought of displaying the martial arts, he has the disease of the martial arts. If an archer is possessed by the thought of shooting an arrow, he has the disease of archery. Only with your ordinary state of mind can you control your sword or your bow and arrow freely.

A natural mind is most important. If you try to speak without this state of mind, your voice will tremble. If you try to draw letters in the presence of other people and lose your ordinary mind, your hand will tremble and write illegible marks. Many Confucians somehow fail to understand the truth of such an open mind. They are solely obsessed by the idea of kei. Kei is hardly the highest state of mind to reach. Indeed, it is an earlier state of the whole process of mental training.

Shin Gan

ITTOSAI SENSEI KENPO-SHO

Technical Study of Kenpo

By Kotoda Yahei Toshisada

"When the soul and the sword become one,
one will be able to adapt freely to any situation."

THE ITTOSAI STYLE was originated by Itou Ittosai Kagehisa. General information on his life is unknown and leaves some mysterious questions unanswered. None of the systematic commentaries written by masters of the early Itto school have survived.

According to the Honchoubugeishouden (Imperial Court Martial Arts Biography Sketch) written in 1716, he was born in Izu and mastered the Chyuujiyou-style sword art under Kanemaki Jisai. He traveled to other lands and challenged other martial artists to fights to the death on 33 separate occasions. It is recorded that his style was divine to the point of indescribable.

The author of this volume, Toshisada, was the grandson of Toshinao, a retainer in the Odawara House of Hojo, Toshinao studied under Itou when Itou visited this house. Toshinao compiled the teachings of Ittosai into the "Teacher Ittosai Sword Manual," written half a century after Ittosai's time, when the world was at relative peace. At this time, the pursuit of justice and morality had become neglected and was replaced by empty theorizing. To pass on the true theories and skills of the sword in such times, Toshisada put to paper the oral instructions of Ittosai in the "Teacher Ittosai Sword Manual." The author warned in writing of the trends of his times against the tendency of many swordsmen to discuss only impractical theories instead of attending to the more difficult task of actually training. Although theory and technique are like the wheels on two sides of a vehicle, the author said, "Physical training and learning of techniques should come first."

According to conjecture by some of Toshisada's followers, Toshisada served the Toda family of the Mino Ogaki clan during the latter part of his life. He lived sometime during the lifetimes of Yagyu Muneyoshi and Yagyu Munenori (son of Muneyoshi).

Toshisada believed that the core of training lies in the basics. He talked about how the pursuit of justice and morality is important, and how the basics are of utmost importance. One cannot find the way of the sword by abstract theorizing. While these writings focus on the use of the sword, it is important to realize that sword or weapon practice, as well as empty-hand martial arts practice, is a basic means to begin to focus one's energies and inner strength for accomplishing a wide variety of difficult tasks in all aspects of life.

Uchu

SKILL AND REASON

The core of the sword is skill.

Skill accomplishes reason.

Make the training of skill be number one.

Grasp the workings of the mind and body—the strengths and weaknesses, the lightness and heaviness, and the advance and retreat.

Understand the reason to change one's techniques in response to the workings of one's opponent.

Victory comes from practicing skill and reasoning.

Whether together or apart, skill and reasoning have to be established in order for one to respond to one's opponent.

For skill to come alive, the mind and the sword must work together as one.

In order to utilize the understanding of the nature of reason and the heart and responding to one's opponent, it is essential to accumulate personal experience.

TRUE VICTORY SURPASSES SKILL AND REASON

A fight lies in the change of technique.

Apply techniques that are beyond the opponent's anticipation.

When the opponent makes a challenge, defend oneself.

The opponent and oneself act and think the same way.

All situations follow nature's laws—respond by transforming oneself.

Become one with the opponent, like an image reflected in a mirror.

The more one aims to win, the more one is likely to ail.

When one has no notion of winning, one cannot lose.

While losing a fight is obviously not one's goal, being concerned only about winning is also not the natural state.

Surpass the superiority, or inferiority, of skill.

Aspire to higher dimensions. People who have accomplished this are no longer adversaries.

One who moves toward the opponent destroys oneself.

One who does not move toward the opponent is also destroyed.

When mind and skill become one, determining victory or

defeat becomes irrelevant.

Possess both heart and skill and be of service to all people. To that end, establish a moral superiority.

When this stage is reached, the murderous sword becomes the living sword.

WRITINGS ON THE
FENCING SCHOOL OF ZUISHIN

A swordsman must know his own weakness in light of those of his opponent. The situations under which he can be defeated are the ones in which his opponent can win. The situations in which he cannot win are the ones in which his opponent has guarded himself well. If he doesn't force himself to win, he will not be defeated. At the same time, there is no victory unless he is prepared for defeat, for in the expectation of victory resides the potential for defeat. A great swordsman experiencing success is also aware of the conditions of defeat; when losing, he can grasp the conditions for victory. If superiority is the result of a realistic estimation of his strength, then inferiority is the result of the inability to perceive reality and a lack of courage and intellect. A victorious person in this life is not a superman but one who, while knowing which conditions are the causes of failure, also knows which conditions are the causes of success.

Overpower with Dignity and Win with Forcefulness

Dignity is not circumstantial. Dignity is a state in which a person's preparation is both determined and correct and in which he cannot be influenced at all by the opponent. Dignity is being able to overpower one's opponent without having to make a move, while immobility is not being controlled by one's opponent. Forcefulness is being able to overpower one's opponent through one's maneuvers. Flexibility is being able to adjust one's actions according to the situation. Dignity may appear peaceful, but within it is concealed the ability to change and fit any situation. Forcefulness, too, can alter itself in many ways when in motion. Face the opponent with dignity and win through strength. Dignity is found in strength, and strength is found in dignity.

Reflecting about Intuitiveness in Practice

The technique of adapting to circumstances is not achieved by utilizing the conscious mind; it is necessary to adjust intuitively, according to natural laws, without having to calculate one's movements. One should respect this power within oneself. Believe in victory without thoughts of futility and endeavor to achieve "correct" revelations. If one wishes to achieve the highest state, there will be no need to worry about matters that will disarray the soul, nor any need to guard the soul. The soul and the body will become one; distinctions between good and evil will not exist. One will possess the knowledge of the function of the sword; one will freely be able to react to any situation. Although attempts are made to teach this highest state, it is impossible. This state of the soul and the body is one that can be achieved only after ceaseless practice. When one has achieved this state, one will be able to adjust to all situations unconsciously.

Skill in Striking First

If one attacks with a frontal strike, the enemy will always utilize surprise tactics or attempt a counterattack. In reverse, in making a counterattack, the opponent will always respond with a frontal attack, so one must always be prepared with the proper defensive form.

Skill in Withstanding Attacks

If the opponent is stirred beneath a calm appearance, take advantage of his unsettled state. If his spiritual state is calm but he appears agitated, oppose him without exerting all your strength. When both the soul and the appearance are agitated, strike at this weak moment; when both the soul and the appearance are not agitated, wait for the moment when one of them weakens. If one's movements are controlled by the opponent's actions, then one is susceptible to danger. Having one's thinking technique controlled by the opponent makes it impossible to win, or even to withstand the opponent's attack. The opponent is confronted by utilizing one's body or one's physical strength skillfully, and confronting the opponent's technique by utilizing a calm spirit. One can destroy the opponent by confronting him and also by confronting his technique. Through practice of technique, one learns the nature of the sword, the pointers about attack, the fundamentals and flexibility in the use of the sword, and the relationship between the sword and the fencer. When the soul and the sword become one, one will be able to adapt freely to any situation.

BEING CONCERNED ABOUT MA
(INTERVALS OF TIME)

The essence of victory is determined in these moments of time, or *ma*. Ma consists of the relationship between two people, the rhythm of the match, and the ability to utilize the existing tempo advantageously. Without allowing the opponent to take an advantage, or even have time to think about the dangerous situation, one should be able to stealthily seize the power of determining life and death. If one is conscious of this interval of time, then one will not be able to move freely. Only if one is not conscious of this interval is one able to utilize it correctly. Not having ma entrapped in the soul or the soul in ma means having achieved the state of *suigetsu*, or having surpassed either technique or rationale. Still being conscious of technique and rationale means not having achieved this state. If the cloud in one's soul vanishes and everything becomes suigetsu, then nothing is impossible. Ma is not spatial distance between the opponent and oneself but encompasses everything that exists. It is being able to decide in the moment and react reflexively.

Winning by Reacting to the Opponent's Initial Moves

One method of winning is to base one's tactics on the opponent's tactics. If the opponent utilizes the frontal attack, attack from the front; if he makes a surprise attack, then return it likewise. If the opponent appears strong yet conceals weakness, then one should appear weak. (The usual pattern is to use surprise: if the opponent attacks directly, one counterattacks indirectly, and vice versa. This is the reverse of the previous statement.)

If both the opponent and oneself have penetrated the mystery of the art, then the soul and technique have become one, and the matter of winning or losing is irrelevant. Determining which sword is superior for one's own satisfaction is not the purpose of the confrontation; through it one saves lives.

FUDOCHI SHINMYO ROKU
The Miracle of Immovable Wisdom

By Takuan Soho

"The scarecrow has no mind but serves its function well."

THE MIRACLE OF Immovable Wisdom (Fudochi Shinmyo Roku) *was written by Takuan Soho (1573–1645). He was a leader of priests in Kyoto at the age of thirty-five, but was exiled because he advocated the independence of religion from the shogunate government. Years later, he was allowed to return by Yagyu Munenori, who was an advisor of the third shogun. He then lectured for the shogun about Zen.*

Takuan Soho wrote this volume at Munenori's request. It contains ideas remarkably similar to those in Munenori's Hei-Ho-Kaden-Sho *(which extended* Fudochi Shinmyo Roku *to the military arts—and is included elsewhere within this book).*

The author's writings are presented in their original form, as a narrative or discussion. He expounds on the nature of human life and the path to self-realization by discussing key points in sword strategy. Fudochi Shinmyo Roku *emphasizes the importance of combining mental and physical training. It presents the importance of applying oneself fully to achieve success at various endeavors, including a military artist, a politician, a parent, and a master.*

As with many masters, Takuan Soho was well versed in many arts, including calligraphy, haiku, and the tea ceremony. To this day, his name is used for the pickled daikon radish, which he developed.

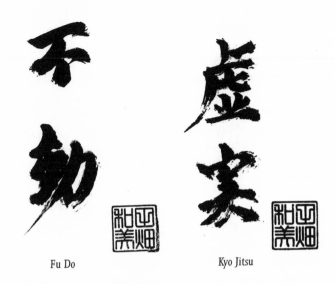

Fu Do

Kyo Jitsu

MUMYO JUCHI BONNO: WHEN THE MIND STOPS, DELUSION ARISES

Mumyo means "not clear" and refers to delusion, doubt, or vacillation. Ju means to stop; in this case it means stopping the mind on everything. Juchi indicates the state in which the mind has stopped. In Buddhist training, there are fifty-two stages, and juchi refers to the stage in which the mind attaches itself to everything it encounters.

I will explain this in terms of your strategy. As your opponent attacks you with his sword and you immediately try to strike back, if your mind is caught, even slightly, by your opponent's sword, you will falter and be instantly cut down by your opponent. This is what is meant by "stopping." However, suppose that, even though you see the opponent's sword cutting towards you, you do not "stop" in your mind, but without any thoughts of trying to return your opponent's strike, you leap right into him, seize his sword, and wrest it away. Then you can turn the sword that would have killed you into its opposite, a sword that will kill your opponent.

In Zen, this is known as "taking the enemy's spear and killing him with it." The "spear" could be any weapon.

If you place your mind on the sword, it will be caught by the sword. If you concentrate on timing and distance, your mind will be caught by timing and distance. Then your actions will be futile, and you will be killed by your opponent.

It is not good to pay attention to your opponent's mind or to place your attention on your own body. Putting the mind on one's own body is a temporary stage of the beginning student.

Whenever the mind is captivated, this means it has stopped and you have become like an empty shell. I think you must have had this experience. In Buddhist terms, the mind-that-stops is called *mayoi*: delusion.

SHOBUTSU FUDOCHI (IMMOVABLE BUDDHA WISDOM): NOT STOPPING THE MIND ALLOWS IT TO BE COMPLETELY USEFUL

Fudo literally means unmoving or immovable, but this does not mean lifeless like a stone or a piece of wood. *Fudochi* (immovable wisdom) indicates the state in which the mind does not stop and can move freely forward, backward, right, left, or in any direction.

Fudomyoo is the name of a Buddhist guardian deity who is usually shown gripping a sword in his right hand and a rope in his left, baring his teeth and glaring ferociously. He stands ready to defeat any evil spirits obstructing Buddhism. This is a symbolic representation of fudochi, which protects the true law of Buddhism. The fearful nature of this manifestation of fudochi causes the common people to respect and uphold Buddhist teachings. In people who are approaching enlightenment, this figure brings about the realization that through perseverance in spiritual training they can, like Fudomyoo, triumph over wickedness or obstructions of any sort. In other words, the figure of Fudomyoo expresses the immovable aspect of the human mind.

If your mind "stops" on something, judgments of various sorts appear and thoughts race about busily within the mind. A mind that stops like this—a mind of attachment—cannot be made to move again. But let us say that you are under attack by ten opponents with swords. You can take on all ten successfully if, after dodging the first sword cut, you do not allow your mind to "stop" on it but instead move freely from one person to the next. This means that, if you are facing ten opponents, you must move your mind ten times. If your mind does not become attached to any one of them, you will be able to fight all of them one after another. However, if you allow the mind to "stop" on one opponent, even if you are able to parry his sword, you will move carelessly when a second person attacks.

Kannon Bosatsu (the Buddha who is the personification of compassion) is sometimes depicted as having a thousand arms. Each one holds something different, such as a bow, a spear, or a sword. If the mind of Kannon Bosatsu "stops" on the arm holding the bow, the other 999 arms are rendered useless. However, not stopping the mind allows all one thousand arms to be of use.

THE HIGHEST STATE IS TO RETURN

At the highest level, one returns to the mind of the beginner. From the beginning states of practice one advances through various different levels, and when the state of fudochi is reached, one returns once again to the first state of mushin (no mind).

Let me explain this in terms of your strategy. When you are a beginner, you know nothing of how to hold the sword or what stances to take; consequently, your mind does not "stop" on your own body; you simply respond to your opponent's sword without any conscious planning. But after receiving instruction in technique, having been taught various stances, methods of disarming your opponent, ways to concentrate the mind, and so on, your mind "stops" on all sorts of things. When you have the intention to strike your opponent, other thoughts arise in your mind and interfere with your ability to carry out your plan. But as the days and months of training go by, you will find yourself able to stand and hold the sword without losing the state of mushin—the same state of mind as the beginner who has had no training.

What does this mean? The state of mind at the beginning and at the end at the same time. It is as if you have counted from one to ten in a cycle, and the first and last numbers rest side by side. In musical scales as well, when you start with the lowest note and gradually raise the pitch, the highest and lowest notes correspond to each other.

This is also true in Buddhism. When a person attains deep understanding, all ostentatious show of this attainment drops completely away. The mumyo and bonno of the beginning stage merge with the fudochi, which has resulted from training, and a perfect clarity of mind (mushin munen, no mind, no thoughts) can be reached. Ultimately, the hands and feet move as if on their own and do not distract the mind at all.

THE SCARECROW

The Zen priest Butukoko Kokushi wrote a poem that expresses this idea of mushin:

> The scarecrow has no thought of protecting the rice seedlings, but birds and beasts see a human figure holding a bow and arrows and flee in fear. . . . The scarecrow has no mind but serves its function well.

A person who has reached a level of mastery in any discipline may be compared to the scarecrow. Although his whole body may be moving, his mind is not caught in any one place, and a state of complete clarity and absence of thoughts (munen mushin) can be reached.

It is the same in all fields. Ordinary untrained people lack knowledge from the outset and thus do not make an outward display of wisdom. Similarly, people who have attained high levels of understanding do not show their wisdom outwardly. Strangely enough, it is those who have only superficial knowledge of things who cultivate an appearance of wisdom. I am ashamed to say that recently you can see this absurd condition even among priests.

TECHNIQUE AND PRINCIPLES REPRESENT TWO WHEELS OF A CART

We can distinguish between the study of principle and the study of technique. The study of "principle" means training that is aimed at reaching the highest state—mushin—in which the mind is set free and is not "caught" by anything at all. However, even if you have an intuitive understanding of principle, you will not be able to move your body properly without also practicing technique. In terms of your strategy, the study of technique means mastering the five basic stances and various other methods of practice. A mere knowledge of theory will not enable you to execute techniques at will. On the other hand, an awesome sword style will be of no use unless you have achieved a grasp of the processes involved through the study of principles. Technique and principle are like two wheels on a single cart.

NOT EVEN A HAIRSBREADTH INTERVAL

Let us examine the saying "not even a hairsbreadth interval" in terms of strategy. "Interval" refers to a space or a gap. The saying describes two things that are so close together that not even a single strand of hair can be placed between them. For instance, if you clasp your hands, a sound comes out without delay at the instance of the clap; there is not a hairsbreadth interval between the clap and the sound. The sound does not take time to pause and think before emerging but comes out instantaneously. If your mind "stops" on your opponent's sword as it cuts towards you, a gap appears. The existence of a gap means that you are open and vulnerable to your opponent's attack. However, if there is not even a hairsbreadth gap between the opponent's sword cut and your own movement, his sword becomes the same as your own.

The same kind of attitude is employed in Zen question and answer sessions. In Buddhism, if the mind does not move freely but lingers on each thing, it is criticized as bonno, a mind disturbed by desire. It is important that the mind move spontaneously and flow onward without the slightest pause, like the movement of a ball dropped into a swiftly flowing stream.

IT IS ESSENTIAL NOT TO STOP THE MIND

There is a saying, "spark from a flintstone," which means essentially the same thing as "not even a hairsbreadth interval." When the flint strikes steel, a spark is immediately produced. There is no gap between the striking of the flint and the emergence of the spark. In the same way, there must not be any gap caused by the stopping of the mind. This must not be misunderstood to mean speed or agility. The important thing is not to stop the mind on anything. Ultimately, speed results from not stopping the mind. This is an essential point. If you stop your mind, it will be captured by your opponent. If you move with the intention to be quick, your mind will be caught by your own intention.

In Saigyo's anthology of poems there is one by a courtesan of Eguchi that reads as follows:

> *Some people loathe this world, but after all it is only a temporary lodging—you must not stop your mind long enough to detest it.*

The latter part of the poem, "You must not stop your mind" expresses the essence of strategy. Not stopping the mind is truly essential.

If you ask a Zen priest, "What is the Buddha?" he may raise his fist. If you ask, "What is the essence of Buddhism?" the priest is likely to respond, "A spray of plum blossoms" or "The oak tree in the garden," even before the sound of your question has died away. Whether the answer is "good" or "bad" is not important. What is valued is the free and spontaneous movement of the mind. A mind that does not stop is not influenced by color or scent. This unwavering mind can be called God, Buddha, the spirit of Zen, or the essence of any art. If you pause to deliberate before responding to a question, your words may be splendid but your mind is obscured by hesitation and doubt. This is known as *mayoi*.

MASTERING FUDOCHI

The saying "spark from a flintstone" also indicates lightning speed. For example, if the name "Uemon" is called and Uemon responds immediately with "Yes," that is fudochi. If upon hearing his name called, Uemon first ponders what the person might want of him and then says something like, "What is it?" that is due to hesitation of mayoi in the mind. The mind of an ordinary person is moved and bewildered by external things, which indicates it is stopped by mayoi. Uemon's immediate response to his name being called is "Buddha wisdom." Buddha and humanity are not two separate things. Attaining this state of mind, that is, completely mastering fudochi, can be called God or Buddha. There are many paths—the way of the gods (Shindo), the way of poetry, the way of Confucius, and so on, but the essence of all of them is realizing the state of mind of fudochi.

UNDERSTANDING THE MIND

When the mind is explained in words, we talk about its universality and its relationship to "karma" (the law of cause and effect). Good will and evil depend on the karma of the mind, and all actions are caused by karma. But what is this "mind"? Everyone is perplexed as to the true nature of the mind.

There are very few people who have a clear understanding of the mind. Even if they understand it, it is even more difficult to put that understanding into action. The ability to explain what the mind is does not mean one has clearly probed its depths. An explanation of water does not moisten the mouth. Even a thorough explanation of fire does not make the mouth hot. A real understanding only comes after you have actually touched water and fire. An empty stomach is never filled by words, no matter how eloquent. Skill with words does not indicate real knowledge, and you cannot achieve an understanding through the explanations of one who thinks he can explain.

It is generally thought that Buddhism and Confucianism teach the nature of the mind. However, if the actions of the teacher are not consistent with what is being taught, this indicates an incomplete understanding. For a complete understanding, it is necessary to have penetrated to the very essence of your own mind. It does not matter how many people study Buddhism if those who have studied do not have a clear grasp of the mind. The attitude of people studying Buddhism is not very good in this regard. The only way to achieve a clear understanding of the mind is through deep thought and extreme, total effort.

WHERE SHOULD ONE PUT THE MIND?

If you put your mind on the movements of your opponent's body, your mind will be captured by them. If you focus your mind on your opponent's sword, your mind will be taken by the sword. If you concentrate on trying not to cut your enemy, your mind will be caught by the thought of cutting. If you put your mind on your own sword, it will be made a captive by your own sword. If you fix the mind on the thought that you must not be cut, your mind will be captured by that thought. If you put your mind on your opponent's stance, your mind will be taken by your opponent's stance. It seems there is no place at all to put the mind.

If you direct the mind towards something outside of yourself, it will be captured by its destination and you will be defeated. Therefore, some people say that you should push the mind down below your own navel and keep it there while moving in response to your opponent's movements. This is a reasonable thing to say. However, from the perspective of the ultimate state of mind in Buddhism, keeping the mind below the navel is a relatively low level of consciousness and cannot be called the ultimate. It is just one state of mind that facilitates the attainment of a certain level of training. It corresponds to the state of kei (reverence). When Mencius said to "bring back the liberated mind (the mind that has separated from you)," he was referring to this level of consciousness, but it is not the highest state.

I believe you will understand this concept of the "liberated mind" by what I have written in other chapters. If you push the mind down below the navel and attempt to keep it there, your mind will be captured by the thought of preventing its escape. You will be unable to do anything more than that, and the movement of the mind will be restricted.

If keeping the mind below the navel destroys one's freedom of movement, then in what part of the body should the mind be kept? If you put the mind in your right hand, it will be captured by the right hand, and your body will be unable to move freely. If you put the mind in the eyes, it will be caught by the eyes, and the movement of the body will be restricted. If you put the mind in your right leg, it will be stuck in the right leg, and again the body will experience difficulty in moving. If you try to put the mind in any one place, then it is absent from all the other places.

Then where should you put the mind? This is my answer: you must not put the mind anywhere. Then it will expand out to fill the entire body.

When the hands are needed, the mind will serve the hands. When the legs are needed, the mind will serve the legs. When the eyes are needed, the mind will serve the eyes. Since the mind extends out to all places, it is able to be where it is needed and perform actions as they become necessary.

If you single out one place in which to keep the mind, it will be caught by that place and become useless. When you think, the mind is seized by your own thought. Throw away your thoughts and judgments—throw away your entire mind. If you do not attempt to keep the mind in any specific place, it will expand to fill the entire body and will not fail to be of service.

If the Mind Is Not Put in One Place, It Is Everywhere

Putting the mind in one place indicates a lapse into one-sidedness or partiality (hen). A proper state of mind is one in which the mind does not concentrate on one side but penetrates the entire body and is extended in all directions. When the mind leans in one direction, it is lacking in all other directions; this is called henshin: a one-sided or biased mind. This sort of bias is rightly detested. Any fixed condition lapses into one-sidedness and leaves the path of righteousness.

If you do not think about where to put the mind, it will expand and extend to all places. Without placing the mind anywhere, move with your opponent and use the mind appropriately in each time and place. If the mind has expanded out to fill the entire body, when the hands are needed you can use the part of the mind that is already in the hands; when the legs must move, the mind is already there. On the other hand, if the mind is fixed in one place, when it is needed in another place, it must first be pulled away from its location. This ties up the attention in that place and the mind becomes useless.

If you try to hold the mind back like a cat on a leash, the mind will be captured by the body. If you let it move freely within the body, it will not escape. Not stopping the mind in one place is the essential point of all training. If you do not put the mind anywhere, it is everywhere. If it is not fixated on one direction, it can function in all directions.

Honshin (Original Mind) Is Like Water; Moshin (Mind of Delusion) Is Like Ice.

The original mind (honshin) never stops in one place but expands throughout the body. The moshin (mind of delusion) is consumed by thought and has become fixated in one place. When the original mind concentrates in one place, it turns into the mind of delusion. It is essential not to lose your original mind, because if it is lost there will be times when your mind will be of no use.

The original mind is like water, and the mind of delusion, which has hardened into one place, is like ice. Water and ice are essentially the same thing. You cannot wash your face and hands with ice, but if you melt the ice into water and let it flow freely, you can wash anything with it. If a person's mind freezes in one place, it cannot be used freely, just as you cannot wash your hands with ice. Dissolve the hardness in the mind, feel as if water were spreading and flowing throughout your body, and use the mind in complete freedom. This is called honshin.

Attaining the State of Mushin

The mind of mushin (no mind) is similar to honshin, the original mind. It does not harden or stop, and it contains no thoughts or judgments. It does not rest anywhere but expands freely through the body. If the mind stops, thoughts arise. If the mind does not stop, it remains empty; this is the mind of mushin. This is also called mushin munen (no mind, no thought).

If you are able to attain the mind of mushin, your mind will respond to everything but stop on nothing. It is as if the mind constantly flowed like water throughout the whole body. In this state you can move freely when necessary.

A mind that is fixed in one place cannot move freely. A wheel turns because it is not tightly attached to the axle. It is the same with the mind.

If there are thoughts in your mind, you will not be able to hear what a person is saying even if you listen, because your mind will stop on your own thoughts. If your mind is biased in the direction of your own thoughts, you will listen without hearing and look without seeing. This is because there are thoughts in the mind.

If you eliminate the thoughts in your mind, you will achieve mushin, and you will be able to move freely and appropriately. On the other hand, the intention to eliminate the thoughts in the mind becomes yet another thought. If you do not particularly try to think, the thoughts will vanish naturally. If you practice this continuously, in the end the mind will spontaneously reach the state of mushin.

Utilize the Mind without Stopping It

In any endeavor, if you have the intention to employ a technique, your mind will be caught by the technique. You must utilize your mind without allowing it to be caught.

You must utilize the mind in order to make use of the hand. Wherever the mind goes, there it stops. A person in any discipline who can utilize the mind and employ techniques without stopping the mind can be called a master.

Attachment and the suffering of life and death are born from the stopping of the mind. The highest state of mind is one in which you can look at flowers or red autumn leaves and see them without stopping your mind. The priest Jien wrote a poem expressing this:

> Although the flowers gave off their fragrance unconsciously,
> my mind stopped on them . . .
> how regrettable

Whether looking or listening, the highest state is not stopping the mind.

Like a Gourd Floating on Water

If you push or strike a gourd floating on water, it will rotate. If you throw a gourd into water and push on it with your hand, the gourd will pop to one side. If you push again it will escape again. It never stays in one place. The mind of a person who has reached a high level of consciousness does not stop for a moment; it is like a gourd floating on water.

The Mind of Kei (Reverence) Is One-Pointed Concentration

In neo-Confucianism, the concept of reverence (kei) is explained as unifying the mind on one point. This means putting the mind in one place and keeping it there. In sword work as well, when you draw the sword and cut with it, the principal objective is to keep the mind from going off in the direction of the cut. The mind of kei is especially important when you receive orders from your lord.

There is also a state of kei in Buddhism. At the beginning of a memorial service, a bell is rung three times, and the hands are brought together in prayer to Buddha. The mind is then unified and the attention is focused into a complete one-pointedness. This is similar to the state of kei.

Kei

LETTING THE MIND GO WHERE IT WANTS TO GO
In Buddhism, kei is not the highest state of mind. It is merely a stage in the process of training the mind to be undisturbed. After years of training the mind to be undisturbed, you can reach the state in which you can send the mind in any direction and still utilize it freely. This is the highest state of mind. In the state of mind called kei, the mind is not given its freedom. You think that if you release the mind it will fall into disorder, so you attempt to hold it in one place, and you are never off your guard. This is "training an undisturbed mind."

But it is inconvenient if one is always in this state. It is as if, for example, a cat were tied up with a rope and kept in one place because it once caught a baby sparrow. If you tie your mind up like a cat on a rope, you will be unable to use it freely. But if you train the cat well, you can untie the rope and let it go wherever it wants. The cat will be able to coexist with sparrows and not catch them. The mind must be set free and, like an unleashed cat, be allowed to travel wherever it wants to go; but it is essential that it not stop in one place.

Applying this to strategy, you must not stop the mind on the hand holding the sword. You must completely forget about the hand and simply cut. Understand that your opponent is empty, you yourself are empty, the moment of cutting and the sword that cuts are also empty. Furthermore, do not let your mind get stuck on the idea of emptiness.

Zen

CUTTING THE SPRING BREEZE IN A FLASH OF LIGHTNING

It is said that when the Zen priest Mugaku was captured and about to be killed by Mongol soldiers, he recited the words,

The spring breeze is cut in a flash of lightning

Hearing this, the soldiers threw down their swords and fled. In the mind of the Zen teacher, the mind raising the sword overhead was the same as a flash of lightning. There was no mind in the person who cut, no mind in the raised sword, and no mind in the one about to be cut. The person wielding the sword, the sword, and Mugaku himself were all empty. The person striking was not a person. The striking sword was not a sword. He himself, facing death, was like the wind that blows across the spring sky. The mind of the Zen teacher did not stop on anything. He would not have resisted even if the sword had "cut the wind."

This is the state of the mind of a master. The mind is completely forgotten, yet all actions are carried out. It is the same in dance. If you try to make your movements look good, or if you have the intention to dance skillfully, you cannot yet be called a master.

All of the arts lose their interest if the mind is stopped on the hands and feet. For a technique to be good, the mind must be completely abandoned.

Pursue the Liberated Mind
Mencius said, "Pursue the liberated mind." This means that when your mind is released and separates from your body, you must pursue it and bring it back. When a dog, a cat, or chicken escapes, you search for it and bring it back. When the mind, which is supposedly attached to the body, gets away from you, you should be able to bring it back. This is a logical point of view.

However, the philosopher Shokosetsu held a completely different view. He said that the main point was liberating the mind. Shokosetsu explained that if you tie up the mind within your own body, it will be like a pet cat, and your original, free mind will be unable to move. You must train the mind not to stop or indulge in things and then set it free.

Bringing the mind back to one's own body and not allowing it to stop due to the influence of external things is a guideline for practice at the beginning level. The lotus spreads its roots in a bog, but its flower is never stained by the mud. A well-polished crystal can be dropped in the mud without being stained by it. Make your mind like the unstainable crystal and then let it go where it wants. Constant tight restraint cripples the mind. Restraining the mind is a beginning stage of training. If you go on training with this attitude forever, even if you train to the best of your ability, you will not reach the higher levels of mastery. You will spend the rest of your life on the level of the beginning student.

At one stage of practice, Mencius' advice, "Pursue the liberated mind," is important. But in order to reach the higher levels it is as Shokosetsu said: "The main point is liberating the mind."

The priest Chuho said, "Arm yourself with a liberated mind." This is the same as Shokosetsu's advice to free the mind. You must not attempt to keep the mind in one place. Chuho also said, "Have an unchanging mind without distractions." This means that you must not let the mind become sloppy. You must grasp the state of mind that will not become distracted even if you are exhausted or faced with an emergency.

A Ball Thrown into Rapids

There is a saying, "A ball thrown into rapids never stays in one place." If you throw a ball into churning rapids, it will ride the waves and dance on the surface of the water. Drawn along by the current, the ball will not stop moving for even an instant. So it is with the mind: it must not stop for an instant even under the most trying circumstances.

Treasure Your Short Life

The life of a morning glory flower is short and fresh. By the time the sun is high in the sky and white summer clouds have formed, the flower has already wilted. Human life is like the morning glory flower. Life is fleeting and should be lived with great care.

Separate the Past from the Present

It is not good to hold on to one's previous thoughts or to retain what is presently in the mind. You must make a clean and complete cut between the past and the present. If the mind is drawn off into thoughts of the past, that means it has stopped. It is important that the past does not interfere with the present, so cut off your previous thoughts and be careful not to stop your mind.

ESTABLISHING PEACE IN THE NATION AND AMONG PEOPLE

The following is presented in the original narrative from the author of this chapter.

I would like to say what has been on my mind. It is only my humble opinion, but I will take this opportunity to write it down for you.

You are a master of strategy unequalled in history, so presently your rank and income are high and your reputation in society is tremendous. Whether waking or sleeping, you must never forget your debt of gratitude for the kind treatment you have received. From morning to night, please think only of serving the shogun with complete loyalty.

Serving with complete loyalty means first of all correcting your own mind, behaving modestly, and never entertaining thoughts of disobeying the shogun. It also means you must not blame or bear resentment towards others. You must apply yourself seriously to your work, serve your parents with filial piety, behave with propriety towards your wife, and not love another woman or get carried away by sexual desire.

Furthermore, as a parent you should conduct yourself with dignity and in accordance with what is right. When dealing with your subordinates, be fair and impartial. Employ people of virtue and use them well. It is important for you to reflect on your own deficiencies, rule your domains justly, and keep your distance from unvirtuous people.

Your doing so will allow good people to become more virtuous day by day, and bad people, influenced by their master's devotion to virtue, will gradually abandon evil and turn towards the good. In this way, if both the lord and the subjects, the higher and the lower, are virtuous, lack greed, and avoid extravagance, the domain will prosper, the people will become affluent, and all will be well. If children have affection in the heart towards their parents and the lower works for the higher like the arms and legs serve the head, peace will naturally be established in the land. This is the beginning of loyalty.

If your soldiers have this kind of loyalty, even a company of a million soldiers will obey your commands without fail under any circumstances. This is like the example of the thousand-armed Kannon that I mentioned previously. If the mind of Kannon functions properly, all of the thousand arms are at his command. Similarly, if you have the proper attitude towards military strategy, your sword will move with complete freedom, and thousands of enemy troops will fall under the command of a single sword. This is the greatness of loyalty.

Other people cannot tell whether your state of mind is proper or not. Any plan can be regarded as having good or bad motives behind it. You must carefully consider the merits of any action, and if you then take the good and leave the bad, your mind will naturally become more virtuous. If you are partial to vice, you will not be able to give something up even if you know full well it is bad. If you want to indulge in sexual pleasure and lead a carefree and extravagant life, you will not listen to the suggestions made by good people around you. If a man pleases you, you will promote and favor him even if he is ignorant. If you do not make sure of the virtuous people around you, it is as if they are not there at all. In this state of affairs, you may have thousands of soldiers, but how many will you be able to count on at a crucial time? Young, ignorant, unvirtuous people who have been appointed on the master's whim naturally lack the proper state of mind. They would not think of sacrificing themselves in an emergency. I have never heard of anyone of this frame of mind being of real service to his lord.

When you are selecting students, this sort of unpleasant experience can also occur. This happens if you do not notice that a simple matter of preference has been turned into unvirtuous behavior due to a weak point in your character. Even little things that you think no one will know about will ultimately become widely known. If you, yourself, know something, then all the gods (kami) of heaven and earth are also aware of it, and all people will know as well. Surely it is dangerous to attempt to maintain order in the domain under these conditions.

Regard this sort of situation as one of great disloyalty. Even if you intend to give loyal and passionate service to the shogun, if your own household is in disorder or a rebellion is brewing among the people of your domain, everything will fall into chaos.

It is said that you can judge a person's virtue by his most trusted retainers and close friends. If the lord is virtuous, his closest retainers will also be virtuous. If the Lord is dishonest, his friends and retainers will also be dishonest. If this is the case, the people in the villages will make fun of them, and neighboring domains will hold them in contempt. Likewise, if the lord and his retainers are virtuous, the common people will be satisfied. It is said that virtuous people are the treasures of the country. Please reflect deeply upon the significance of this. If you correct the biased areas in your own mind before they are known to others, stay away from the bad people and cultivate a preference for wise people, the government of the country will set straight, and you will be serving with complete loyalty.

A Parent Must First Correct Himself

In regards to your son's behavior, it is wrong for a parent to scold a child for misdeeds if the parent has not corrected his own mind. You must first of all conduct yourself properly. Then, if you admonish your son, his behavior will improve naturally and your younger son will be sure to learn from his brother's example and improve his behavior as well. It is truly auspicious when father and sons become virtuous together.

When employing or discharging people, base your decisions on loyalty and integrity. Since you are presently a favored retainer, many lords offer you bribes. It would be a terrible thing if you were to be blinded by greed and forget about loyalty. You are also fond of boisterous dancing, and you are overly proud of your own abilities. You visit various lords without an invitation in order to show off your skill. This can only be described as sickness. Furthermore, I hear that you made disparaging remarks about the shogun's poetry, and you were greatly patronized by a lord who flattered you in the presence of the shogun. You must constantly reflect on this sort of thing. In a poem it is said:

> The mind deludes itself. In matters of the mind, you must stay on
> your guard.

Mizu

TAI A KI
The Ultimate Sword

By Takuan Soho

"A true master of strategy gives to others the joy of living and causes them to feel the preciousness of human life."

THE ULTIMATE SWORD (Tai A Ki), along with the preceding chapter, The Miracle of Immovable Wisdom ("Fudochi Shinmyo Roku"), were written by Takuan Soho, Yagyu Munenori's Zen teacher, at Munenori's request.

Tai A was unrivaled as the keenest and most polished sword—to wield such a sword required very high levels of understanding and enlightenment. The chronicles of Tai A were used for kendo instruction in the shogunate. They were recorded and passed down by Ono Jirou Uemon Tadaaki.

The Ultimate Sword (Tai A Ki) deals with one's relationship to others. In it, Takuan explains that the sword must give life, not death. A true master of strategy gives others the joy of living and causes them to feel the preciousness of human life. The Ultimate Sword describes the unceasing effort that must be made in order to become a master of strategy.

Tai A

PRECEPTS OF TAI A

To achieve the polished swordsmanship of Tai A, significant
device and effort are required.

One who has attained Tai A swordmanship is a master of life.

A sword is not a killing weapon.

A strategist who has not achieved the "living sword" is an amateur.

One who excels in swordsmanship but does not excel as a
human being has no value.

Takuan laments the fact that the world is filled with people with
no value.

To become a person of value, one needs to understand and be
able to completely transform oneself.

Actions stem from desires.

Desires should be respected similarly as life.

Desires cannot be killed.

Desires are brought to life depending upon one's wisdom.

Wisdom gives direction to desires.

This wisdom is conveyed to people through Buddhism.

Buddhism creates the path to ponder questions such as, "What
am I?" and "Why are things the way they are?"

A STRATEGIST DOES NOT COMPETE IN FIGHTS

A strategist never competes in fights. Unconcerned with relative strength or weakness, he remains seated and wins over his opponent without taking a single step forward or backward.

THE TRUE SELF AND THE PERSONAL SELF

The true self transcends life and death. It existed before the birth of one's parents. It has been in existence since before the separation of heaven and earth. This self exists in oneself as well as in all things— birds, animals, grasses, and trees. It is called the "Buddha-nature."

The true self has no form and cannot be seen as we ordinarily see things with the eyes. It is perceived by very few. Only those who have completely grasped the way of Buddha, who are enlightened and have attained Buddhahood, can see the true self. The personal self is possessed by ordinary people and is completely visible to others.

The true self does not see "self" and "opponent"; thus, the "opponent" cannot see the "self." To say one does not see "self" and "opponent" does not mean that you do not see the enemy standing before you. You see the figure of the enemy, but you do not look strategically. That is the beauty of it.

ENLIGHTENMENT AND ATTAINING BUDDHAHOOD

A person who has attained Buddhahood is one who has reached enlightenment. Reaching enlightenment means going deeply within oneself to the limits of the mind that is attached to oneself and to external objects. When one fully understands one's mind, that is, that one's original nature is mu (nothingness, void), one immediately becomes a Buddha.

In the past, Shakyamuni Buddha secluded himself in snow-covered mountains, and for six years undertook the severest ascetic practices. After that he attained Buddhahood; he realized his true self. In other words, he realized the self that transcends life and death, the self of mu.

The true self is not something that can be easily or quickly grasped by those who lack strong faith. Those who devote themselves to studying the way of Buddha awaken in themselves the tremendous power of faith, and study diligently for ten or twenty years, maintaining their resolve with the desperate intensity of a parent who has lost a child. Ever-thinking, ever-seeking, and finally arriving at a full understanding of Buddhism, they are able to perceive the true self for the first time. You cannot reach this state by attempting to understand it through intellectual knowledge. You must look directly at that which existed before the creation of heaven and earth, before the differentiation of yin and yang. By doing so, you will surely achieve success.

One Who Has Mastered Strategy

A master of strategy does not kill people with his sword. Anyone standing in front of a master who has realized the truth will naturally cower as if already dead—there is no need to kill him. "Giving life with the sword" means that although you handle the opponent with the sword, you allow him to move as he wishes and you are able to watch freely.

A person who has mastered strategy can give either life or death with complete freedom. If I place a mirror here, it will reflect the form of each thing that is placed in front of it, but the mirror has no mind of its own. It does not make distinctions. It does not think, "this is round, so the reflection must be round," or "I must reflect this square as a square." Similarly, if a person using strategy stands single-mindedly before an opponent, he will have no feeling of distinguishing before good and bad, or strong and weak. Because the mind is free of delusion, he does not see "good" and "not-good." He does not think at all; thus, he understands everything. He walks on water as if it were earth and walks on earth as if it were water. But if a fool tries to walk on water as if it were earth, he will likely fall down even when walking on dry land. If you walk on earth as if it were water, you may feel as if you can actually walk on water. You can realize this truth only if you forget about all things such as earth and water.

This can only be understood by one who clearly knows the original nature of human beings. No number of people can cause trouble for the strategist who has achieved complete freedom of action. One who has reached this state has no peers in this world and stands alone and supreme in the universe.

REACHING THE ULTIMATE STATE

If you aspire to the state of complete freedom of action, then whether you are moving or staying in one place, sitting or lying down, speaking or maintaining silence, drinking tea or eating a meal, you must never be inattentive or slacken in your efforts. You must constantly come back to yourself and look seriously within. As you go on searching, you must try to see the truth in all things whether "good" or "bad." As time passes and you continue your efforts, it will be as if you suddenly encounter a light on a dark night. If you are able to realize this wonderful truth, which will give you complete freedom of action, you will obtain that fundamental wisdom that no teacher can convey to you.

Ordinary people generally perform all their actions self-consciously, and because of this, desires arise and suffering is created. But "action of non-action" emerges spontaneously and without any artificiality. Each action is performed from a place of fundamental wisdom, and consequently it is very relaxed and natural. All of one's actions and behavior become completely free of artificiality. This does not mean that you cease your ordinary activities and behave differently from usual. But it is completely different from the ordinary behavior of a fool. Even if it looks the same, it is different on the inside.

I call this Tai A. Tai A is the name of a famous sword of incomparable excellence. This sword can cut freely through anything, be it as strong as iron or as hard as a stone or a jewel. Nothing in this world can stop it. Likewise, even the general of a great army can do nothing against a person who has realized the miraculous power that I call Tai A: the ultimate sword.

The Ultimate Sword Is within Every Person

This sharp sword, Tai A, which can cut through anything, is not the possession of others. Each human being possesses it; no one lacks it. The "ultimate sword" is a state of mind. This mind is not something that we receive at birth and that ceases to exist when we die. It is our original nature. It is eternal and indestructible. Fire cannot burn it; submerging it in water cannot make it wet. There is nothing in the world that can obstruct the mind.

One who possesses this state of mind can perceive the universe with a clarity of vision that cannot be obstructed. Even evil spirits keep a respectful distance from those who see through every attempt to exercise power. In contrast, the minds of those who do not see their original nature are full of delusive thoughts and can easily be deceived by those who follow evil ways.

If both people in an encounter understand their original nature, and both sides draw, strike, and parry with the sword of Tai A, neither side will be able to defeat the other. It will be like the meeting of Shakyamuni Buddha and his disciple Kasho. Before Shakyamuni Buddha died, he held a single lotus blossom up before the multitudes on Mount Ryoju, but they did not understand its significance and remained silent. Only Kasho comprehended what he was saying and broke into a smile. Upon seeing this, the Buddha knew that Kasho had reached enlightenment, and saying that Kasho had realized the true law that cannot be taught, the Buddha gave Kasho his blessing. Since then, the story of the Buddha's flower and Kasho's smile has come to symbolize telepathic communication, or understanding without words.

However, the teaching of the flower and the smile is extremely difficult to grasp. It cannot be understood by speculation. Even the Buddhas fall silent in awe of this teaching. There is no way to express this truth in words. But if one were forced to try, one would say that when the water in one cup is poured into another cup containing water, the waters mix together until there is no longer any distinction between them. In the same way, the Buddha and Kasho's eyes met and were one. There was absolutely no difference between one and the other. There may not be one in a hundred thousand skillful strategists who truly understands the state of mind indicated by the flower and the smile. If one were born with a tremendous resolve to realize this state of mind, one would need to train oneself intensively for thirty years or more. If one's training took a wrong turn, just as one were about to become a master of strategy, one would surely fall into hell. This is truly a frightening thing.

One Who Has Fully Realized the Buddhist Law of Karma (Cause and Effect)
An intelligent person, upon seeing one action, will predict the second and third developments and can judge quantities and weights accu-

rately with the eyes alone. Many people have this sort of ordinary intelligence. However, one who has fully realized the important Buddhist teaching of karma (the law of cause and effect) will have acted quickly to deal with the third stage of events before even the smallest signs of the first stage have appeared. It is futile to struggle against this sort of person.

For one with this kind of speed, it is so easy to cut with the sword that the opponent's head may fall before he notices. A master at this level does not even seem to draw his sword. His speed is like a flash of lightning; as soon as you see it, it is fading away.

If you are even slightly attached to the lifting of the sword or the place where your mind is focused, you will injure your blade or cut your own hand and cannot be called skillful. It is useless to try to calculate the future, so lay aside your thoughts and calculations and look with an empty mind.

The true strategy cannot be explained in words, and it cannot be taught through instruction in how to stand, where to stroke, and so on. It cannot be communicated through word or gesture. You must realize it yourself, apart from the instruction you receive from your teacher. Then you will be able to act with complete freedom as if there were no rules at all. When you understand and act in accordance with the greater laws, you are free to perform actions in any order at all, and nothing can stand in your way. Even heaven cannot read the mind of one who is able to be so free. Then you have gone beyond all pleasure and pain, and there is no need to try to ward off misfortune, because disasters do not befall you if you have reached this state of completion.

Persevere in your training as if you were a sword to be forged from the purest metal. Then if you reach a full understanding of truth, with one sword you will be able to establish peace in the world. If you want to learn this miraculous truth, you must not stay on the level of simple or coarse teachings, but strive towards a higher and more beautiful spirit, make surpassing effort upon effort, and not waste a moment.

Mu Shin

GORIN-SHO
The School of Two Heavens

By Musashi Miyamoto

"Pay attention to the very smallest of phenomena."

UNLIKE THE OTHER MASTERS, Musashi did not try to put together the principles of Zen and physical techniques of Kempo. Likewise, he did not support the theories of "Divine Protection" like other swordsmen. Instead he organized and systematized the "principles of swordmatch" in his own way, extrapolating from his great many death-match experiences. Musashi mentioned in the book that it could be applicable not only to a man-to-man match, but also to the military arts, and even to the politics of a nation.

Between the ages of thirteen and thirty-nine, Musashi (1584–1646) had over sixty death matches against many different sword fighters. He never lost a single match. He was not only a genius of swordsmanship, but also a master of drawing, poetry (ren-ga), sculpture, and tea ceremony. His book was written in the confines of two years of his life. His book, which is outstanding among secret documents concerning swordsmanship, was completed just weeks before his death at the age of sixty-two.

One who wants to understand budo (Japanese swordsmanship) should study Miyamoto's moral philosophy of the Japanese sword in Gorin-Sho. Budo developed an important moral sense in Japan's feudal period. In Gorin-Sho, Musashi Miyamoto states the principles of fighting matches, which he learned from his own experience at the risk of his life. In contrast, the originators of the other schools gave themselves authority by divine protection by using the theory of Zen in their tactics.

Miyamoto's principles for fighting matches came from his own strategy. He prided himself on their being applicable not only to the individual man-to-man combat, but also to group fighting, and even to the politics of a nation. His fighting tactics in that turbulent age of wars were not only for training the mind, but also for self-defense and consistently defeating the enemy.

One can learn from Gorin-Sho, principles indispensable for the study of karate.

Ken Sei   Gorin-Sho

TO FIND OUT THE USES OF HEI-HO (TACTICS)

Yumi (bow), *teppo* (gun), *yari* (spear), *choto* (long sword), and so on, are kinds of arms, all of which can be used to develop one's tactics. Hei-ho is of special concern in the practice of *tachi* (Japanese samurai sword).

The method of handling the tachi (long sword) is the foundation of tactical knowledge. Thus by mastering it one can govern people and regulate oneself. After mastering the tachi, one can defeat ten enemies; one thousand can defend ten thousand. It will be the same whether one is fighting one enemy or ten thousand enemies.

To master *ken* (sword) and to learn and master all techniques that a master should know well is called hei-ho (strategy). Achieve everything through learning and mastering various techniques. As a human being one should train one's mind and one's ability to the fullest.

Hei Ho

ABOUT RHYTHM AND TEMPO IN HEI-HO

Everything has its own rhythm. In hei-ho, rhythm is especially important, and no one can excel without developing rhythm. That is also applicable to any other military art and technical skill (that is, music, dancing, horse riding, and so on). Naturally, rhythm and tempo must be kept in balance. We also find rhythm and tempo in metaphysical things as in human life. One has suitable rhythm and tempo according to one's prosperity or despair. So it is necessary for one to discover how one's own rhythm depends on development and decline.

There are various rhythms in hei-ho. First of all, one should find out which rhythm will best fit the situation. Then, one should know the extremes of rhythm, fast and slow, light and heavy; furthermore, one should know correct distances and how to disrupt an opponent's rhythm. Without knowing this coordination one cannot master hei-ho. In a storm or a battle, after discovering the rhythm of the enemy, one should meet him with an unexpected rhythm; one can win with such a strategy.

How to Have a Proper View of Hei-Ho

In the battle, you should have a broad view. First, you should clearly ascertain your opponent's ideas of attack and secondly watch his movement. It is important in hei-ho to determine your opponent's true thoughts by catching his distant movements correctly and picking up their essence. Make sure to fix your eyes firmly and yet see to both sides carefully. (Don't look or turn your head, but do see.)

Nine Principles

* Never have a wicked heart.
* Train not by thought, but by practice.
* Learn a wide variety of arts and skills, and do not fix on only one.
* Know not only your own techniques but also those of many others.
* Find out rationally what is an advantage and what is a disadvantage.
* Foster an intuitive ability to judge all things.
* Feel an essence that you cannot see on the surface.
* Pay attention to the very smallest of phenomena. (Everything takes its own course, and sometimes we get unexpected results.)
* Do nothing in vain, for the energy and time we have is limited.

One who always keeps hei-ho in mind and trains vigorously

can be superior to others and also judge matters better than others. The person who comes to control his own body by hard training will have physical strength greater than others. If a person trains his mind in a similar manner, he will then become spiritually superior to others. Accomplishing the above things, he will never be defeated.

How to Keep the Mind in Hei-Ho
In hei-ho, in the case of battle, one has to keep one's mind in its natural state. It is best to eliminate domineering or unnecessary thoughts. We can take proper steps immediately in any situation by keeping the mind calm. Never forget to make your mind work when your body is quiet, and to make your mind calm when your body is in action. It is important to make your mind useful and enrich it with knowledge. Take no account of trifles and thoroughly keep your spirit strong. Never let others detect your true intentions. According to the situation, you must judge matters objectively and make the correct decision no matter what situation you're in. Keep your mind clear and maintain a broad view of things. Train your spirit and improve your knowledge earnestly. You should intend to improve your judgment and keep your spirit calm at all times.

ABOUT BODY FORM IN HEI-HO
The proper forms for your body are as follows:

* You should neither lower your head nor raise it up; just keep it straight.
* Do not stare around restlessly.
* Do not wrinkle your forehead.
* Keep your eyes fixed and narrow and your eyelids open without blinking.
* You should have a peaceful look, with your lower jaw a little pushed forward; keep the rear sinews of your neck straight, harden the nape, and evenly tense the parts of your body below the shoulders.
* Keep your shoulders down and your spine straight; don't push your hips out. Stiffen your legs and feet from the knee to the toe and make your abdomen tense so that your overall body line is straight.

How to Step

In stepping, you should place the heel firmly, raising the toe a little. You should step as you would normally walk, whether your step is wide or narrow, fast or slow. It is wrong to step too fast, unsteadily, or too strongly. You should be careful not to move only one foot at a time. Whenever you go back, attack, or defend yourself, move both feet simultaneously.

To Attack the Enemy at One Beat

You should be in a proper position to cross swords with your enemy. Then, before he judges what to do, you should attack him quickly at one beat, with your body kept quiet and your mind left as it is. To attack the enemy at one beat is to attack him before he makes up his mind. You should learn this one-beat attack, and train to attack as fast as possible.

About a Secondary Attack

In case the enemy should retreat before you attack, you should first pretend to attack, causing your opponent to tense up. Following this tension, your opponent will relax, and you should attack truly without a moment's delay. This is a secondary attack.

About an Attack with Freedom of Thought

In case both you and your opponent are ready to attack at the same time, concentrate to prepare your mind and body thoroughly for the attack. After you decide what technique to use, you should attack strongly with natural acceleration. This is an attack with freedom from all thought.

About Shuko (Monkey with Short Reach)

It is the mental attitude of shuko not to hold out your hands. When you go forward to confront the enemy, you should be careful not to attack with only your hands. If you want to hold out your hands, your body will inevitably come after your hands. Instead, you should swiftly go forward to the enemy with your whole body in order to successfully attack.

To Compare One's Height with the Enemy's

When you come close to your enemy, you should stretch your legs, back, and neck so that you do not shrink. Comparing your height with the enemy's by putting your face and his side by side, you should stretch your body and reflect confidence that you can win. It is necessary to think confidently.

Stabbing from the Front

When your sword and your opponent's are evenly matched, it is fundamental to point your sword at your opponent's face. When you do this, your opponent will try to dodge your attack with both face and body. When he dodges in this fashion, there are several ways in which to achieve victory.

Fighting Many Opponents

This is the technique of one person fighting many opponents. Even when your opponents are attacking from all four directions, this technique enables you to take on those coming from one direction at a time. First, look at the order in which they are attacking, and take on the enemies in the appropriate direction first. Take in a wide field of vision, look at the way in which the opponent is going to attack, fend off his sword, and lunge. After this first lunge, do not hesitate; immediately recover your stance, look to both sides, and lunge in the direction from which the next opponents are attacking. It is extremely important to force your opponents into a straight line. When you perceive that they have formed a line, lunge strongly without hesitating. You will lose your initiative and your efficiency if you always wait for your enemy to attack first. Try to discern the rhythm of the opponents' attack so that you can predict what they will do next; then try to break this rhythm. If you master the technique of dealing with large numbers, you will be able to deal with all opponents with ease, whether you are fighting one, ten, or twenty.

Fighting the Fight to Suit the Surroundings

As a rule, it is always best to stand with your back to the sun. When this is impossible, put the sun at your right shoulder. Even when fighting indoors, make sure the lights are behind you or at your right shoulder, and make certain that there are no obstructions in back of you. Always make certain that you are in a better position than your enemy. Try to move your enemy to your left side. Put your enemy in front of a difficult area and then try to move him backwards. Be careful to keep your enemy occupied so that he cannot look around. Always keep yourself in the more advantageous position.

DISCIPLINE

In mastering the martial arts, you learn the ways in which to defeat an enemy, the use of the sword, good judgment and rhythm, the ways to use your legs and body, and how to make your body more nimble. When you have had the experience of defeating one or two opponents, you will come to understand what constitutes good and bad in the martial arts. Gradually, with practice and experience in handling opponents, you come to understand what the martial arts are about. You will come to understand how to be victorious in battle, and you will become able to discern the psychology of your opponents through fighting a variety of different people. You must be patient. Improvement is a gradual day-by-day process. Today, you will be able to defeat the people who are at the level you were at yesterday. Tomorrow, you will be able to defeat people who are at the level you are at today. Even if you defeat an enemy, you cannot count it as a victory unless you use the principles of mastery. We say, one thousand days of lessons for discipline; ten thousand days of lessons for mastery.

The Three Basic Situations

There are three situations in which to take the initiative.

> Taking the Offensive. There are several ways of attacking. One is to do it quickly and with agility, while maintaining a calm state. Another is to appear strong and fast on the surface while maintaining an internal calm. You can also overwhelm your opponent by becoming tense, approaching quickly, and shouting, or simply empty your mind and concentrate on defeating your opponent.

Defense. When you are attacked, one mode of defense is to remain calm and make yourself appear weak. Then, when the enemy comes near, quickly jump aside, break the rhythm of his attack, and dispatch him in one blow. Show your strength from the beginning. Try to spot the weak points in the attack and take advantage of them.

When You and Your Opponent Take the Offensive at the Same Time. There is a way to take the initiative, even when both you and your opponent attack at the same time. When the opponent attacks in haste, make your own attack quiet. Then, when the opponent nears, move quickly and dispatch him with a strong decisive blow. When the opponent attacks quietly, be fast, look at his approach, and attack him with strength.

These are the three modes of fighting, depending on how you judge the situation at the particular moment. As a rule, under normal conditions, you should attack first. If this is not possible, wait for the enemy to attack, then take control of the situation.

KNOWING YOUR OPPONENT'S STRENGTHS AND WEAKNESSES

Try to find out the particular school of the martial arts your opponent follows. Try to assess his character and judge his strengths and weaknesses. By doing this, you will be able to move so that you can thwart your opponent's intentions. It is important to take the initiative by knowing where he will try a strong or weak attack and by discerning the rhythm of his movements.

Contagion

Many things are contagious. For example, sleepiness and yawning are contagious. During a bout, when your opponent is uneasy and in a hurry, you can entice him to relax by showing that you are unaffected by his uneasy state. When he "catches" your calmness, you can quickly and strongly defeat him. It is important in one-to-one battle to watch for the moment when your enemy becomes lax, because then you can quickly take the initiative. In a sense, you are trying to cast a spell over your opponent. You try to trick him by feigning boredom or weakness. This is a useful tool.

Three Ways to Use Your Voice

There are three ways to use your voice: The scream is used at the beginning, during, and after a bout. This voice is a sign of strength, and it should be able to resound above fire, wind, and ocean waves. At the beginning of a bout you should cry out as loudly as possible. During the bout, lower the pitch of your voice and use a deep cry from the lower chest. After victory, cry out loudly and strongly. These are three ways of using your voice. At the high point in the bout, lower your voice in an effort to overcome your opponent.

THE TECHNIQUE OF ATTACK

Technique is important when you are confronting many opponents. When you have knocked down the opponents coming from one direction or when you have forced them to retreat, take on the opponents coming from another direction and try to grasp the rhythm of their attack. Try to fight in a zig-zag fashion. When you have discerned the abilities of your opponents, press on to a victory without retreating.

The Smash

The smash (hishigu) refers to a situation in which you have found that your enemy is weak, and you defeat him in one strong offensive movement. When your enemy is inexperienced or his rhythm is off or he starts to retreat, you should pursue him without hesitation and smash him with impunity. Never allow him to get back on his feet.

Ku—Knowing the Void

The Japanese word ku can be translated as emptiness, space, sky, air, and so on. The Chinese character for "ku" is the same as the character for the kara in karate. In Chinese and Japanese philosophy the word means more than space or emptiness. It refers to a kind of pristine state of mind, where the mind is empty and pure. It is also sometimes used to describe a pre-rational or a-rational state of matter. Ku penetrates the rational, and pursues and finds the beneficial. Ku refers to the clear interstices between the clouds and despair.

It is said that ku is empty and cannot be known to human beings. But, when we fully understand areas that are not empty, we can for the first time understand areas that are. These are the areas called ku. True ku, or emptiness, is achieved when we achieve a state completely devoid of doubt through daily practice and cultivating our intellect, spiritual power, and abilities to judge. Achieving a state devoid of doubt is the essence of the martial arts. We come to understand true emptiness or ku through committing ourselves to the very maximum amount of training and practice. The mind that achieves ku knows only good and does not know evil. By being endowed with the spirit, knowledge, and truth of the martial arts, the mind that achieves ku is completely without worldly thoughts.

Ku

JYOSEISHI KENDAN

By Matsura Seizan

"The most important part begins even before you put your hand on your sword."

DATEI ZESUIKEN HIDEAKI (1646–1713) was a fore-father of the relatively new Shin Kei To School. This school focused on the common weak points of the human mind and the natural movements of the human body. It taught how to strengthen the mind and body through continual training in order to remain confident under any fighting circumstance. The school flourished for a long time in large part because the most outstanding candidate swordsman succeeded to its leadership, rather than being chosen through family relationship.

An interesting change in philosophy and approach came about during the development of this school. The predecessor to this school, called Hon Shin To Ryu, held as its central tenet that one is seized with fear when one draws a sword for battle, and that despite summoning one's courage, one's true heart remains in fear. True discipline of one's heart must therefore involve recognizing and dealing with this fear.

Eventually, martial arts teachers developed a new philosophy—that continued study of techniques, and the perfection of form, would help to discipline one's heart. Such development would then overcome the desire for victory, freeing one from the need to win or fear of losing. The resulting freedom of mind and spirit would allow one to adapt to any situation. It was this modification of central philosophy that led to the change in name of the school to Shin Kei To Ryu.

This account is attributable to the talents and efforts of author Matsura Seizan. Seizan was a feudal lord in Hizen Hirata.

He was born in 1760 as the thirty-fourth lord of Hizen Hirata, where the Matsura family governed, and was famous for excelling in both swordsmanship and the literary arts.

Hei Jo Shin

TO BE HONEST

If you are honest with yourself, you will recognize that there are two conflicting forces in your heart when you face your opponent. As much as you want to conquer him, you are frightened and you want to avoid him. You must learn to quiet your fear and allow your desire to conquer to flow freely from you.

It is very important that you recognize this fact and train yourself in order to face any opponent without hesitating. This is the real spirit of *honshinto*.

STRIKE YOUR OPPONENT WITH GOD'S POWER

Do not look at your opponent's sword when you strike him. It is desirable that your mind be completely empty. You must ignore all of your thoughts and judgments and react just as dynamite explodes when ignited. Depend on God's power, and strike your opponent with all your might.

Ken Dan

TO BELIEVE

A person who does not believe his master's teaching will never reach a depth of understanding. Likewise, a person who believes every word of his master without question will never reach a depth of understanding.

THERE IS NO MYSTERY OR
SECRET TECHNIQUE IN KEMPO

Occasionally you may be able to win a contest by using unexpected techniques. However, the student who understands the real *kenjutsu* does not rely on mystery.

There are no mysterious techniques using one's hands and feet. Students who are beginners in this field must study hard to understand this truth. The best way to find truth is to engage in real fights as many times as possible.

RESPOND TO ANY CHANGES OF CIRCUMSTANCES

If you fail using one method, do not try to use it again. It is important in Japanese fencing that you make yourself adaptable in many situations. There are certain methods for certain circumstances. Every method that you use has to help bring you victory.

RULES OF FIGHTING

Be ready to fight back whenever you are attacked. You might be at a drinking party or listening to music. Be careful that your enemy doesn't catch you napping.

Get yourself ready before attacking your opponent. Some might think that the most important part of fencing is the actual fighting, but that is not so. The most important part begins even before you put your hand on your sword.

MYSTERIOUS VICTORY

In the world of fighting, there has been a growing tendency toward pseudo-spiritualism. As long as you obey the rules of fighting, you will often be able to win even when you did not expect to. Then you wonder, "How did I manage to win the contest?" The reason is simply that there are no mystical forces at work. All opponents have two arms, two legs, and can be beaten just like yourself. But there is no victory when you ignore the rules or misjudge the techniques of fighting.

IN ONE STRIKE

No matter who your opponent might be, saint or nobleman, do not think of him in that manner. When you face your opponent, cut him down in one strike and think of nothing else.

Think of the dojo as backstage and the backstage as real fighting. Some students think that it is sufficient to do well in the dojo. This is a mistake. In a real fight, you will have no second chance to make up for your mistakes.

When your concentration focuses on cutting your opponent in one strike, the sharpness of the attack will appear as though you were using a real sword. Without this concentration, you lose the sharpness of your skill, and you are just imitating the forms you have been taught. Those who are students of kenjutsu must learn this one thing, it is the most important thing in kenjutsu: discipline! Discipline yourself earnestly in everyday practice. This is the key to victory.

HAVE DIGNITY

You express sorrow when you go to a funeral, and you don't smile within the procession. When a knight puts on armor he becomes very dignified. Likewise, noblemen discipline themselves to be dignified at all times. The students of kenjutsu must think of this when they face opponents. Sharpen your mind and show your dignity.

WHAT IS VICTORY?

A one-time victory is not a lifetime victory. You might beat an opponent one time but not have superiority over him the rest of his life. It is nonsense to judge whether one has earned a real victory in one encounter.

A real victory is a lifetime victory. What is the difference between a one-time and a lifetime victory? In many contests there have been accidental victories, but real victories result after all those accidental elements are eliminated. Often we grow up to misunderstand ourselves; we think that victory arrives because of our excellence and that failure comes accidentally. Thus, the one-time victor may become a lifetime loser.

Chu Do

TENGU GEIZUTSURON

Tengu's Dialogue on the Martial Arts

By Issai Chozanshi

"Precise judgment comes from a mind and a heart that are stable."

ISSAI CHOZANSHI (the pen name of author Tanba Jyuorou-Zaemon Tadaaki, who lived from 1659 to 1741) was a samurai in the domain of Sekiyado who excelled in Zen Buddhism, Confucianism, and Taoism. His widely read work was published in 1729.

The work was organized in the form of a dialogue between a master of the martial arts and some Tengu, who were mountain spirits in Japanese folklore. Legend has it that a man named Ushi-waka-maru learned a secret art from the Tengu, and wielded it to hurt and dominate many. One samurai crept into the mountains to try to learn this secret art on his own. In a blast of wind, a Tengu appeared and revealed the secrets of the martial arts. The dialogue between the Tengu and the samurai covers all of the problems that a person learning the martial arts might encounter.

Tengu

IMPORTANCE OF DISCIPLINE

It becomes more apparent that your body and mind unite and work together as you reach maturity. When you understand this, your mind will be set free, and you will be able to use it any way you want. This has been a doctrine taught in kenjutsu from the beginning.

Therefore, discipline is important for the achievement of maturity in kenjutsu. Your body and mind will not work together if you lack this discipline.

DISCIPLINE YOURSELF
TO GAIN TRUTH AS YOUR OWN

In the old days, he who studied budo had to possess great passion and strong willpower in order to improve his skill. He conditioned himself for hard and faithful training every day. He believed in his master's teachings and studied them day and night. If there were questions, he asked his friends. In this way, he mastered his understanding of the truth. His master did not teach him everything in the beginning, but rather waited for the student to come to understand truth himself.

TRANSCENDENCE OF LIFE AND DEATH

Zen priests set themselves above life and death in order to reach eternal peace of mind. For this reason, it is possible for them to be calm in the midst of enemies, even while being physically attacked. Their philosophy does not keep them from getting killed, but teaches them not to be afraid of death. Not being afraid of death and escaping death are two different things.

PERSISTENCY

You can respond correctly to things around you when your mind is stable; however, an attack on your life is certainly enough to disturb your mind. You might face losing your life, but it is easy to get rid of one's persistency in clinging to life.

WHAT IS THE BEST ATTITUDE?

It is best to have an immovable mind. Only when your mind is stable are you able to make the right judgments of what your reactions should be. Precise judgment comes from a mind and a heart that are stable. You will have the advantage over your opponent if your heart and mind are well prepared.

"Take the initiative" does not necessarily mean to attack your enemy first. The most important thing in kenjutsu is to attack as you defend yourself and to defend yourself as you attack. Whatever the circumstances, prepare to respond promptly.

Sho Shin

SECRETS OF TACTICS

By Kazumi Tabata

"Victory in a match comes from a relaxed state of mind."

THIS BOOK TAKES a fresh look at the classic works on martial arts, strategy, and tactics and presents them in a new way. It combines insights and experiences the author has gained through:

* Oral instruction received when training under Hisao Obata (the leading disciple of Gichin Funakoshi, the Father of Modern Karate) and Isao Tamotsu (originator of Shaolin-style karate).
* His study of judo, kendo, iaido, aikido, jujitsu, kobudo, karate, and other martial arts.
* Research into meditation, religion, visualization, and sports psychology.

We should recognize that the precepts of the old classics also encompass the goals that we seek in the present day. The author considers that the perfection of martial arts is a means to achieve enlightenment. From this vantage point, the study of the sword is similar to practicing a musical instrument for internal development and expression. Only with an undisturbed and tranquil mind can one become capable of the free execution of techniques. This chapter presents approaches for training that will allow a trainee to maintain this state of mind even in the face of overwhelming odds.

Hei Den Sho

THE BASIC PRINCIPLE OF TACTICS

There is a Japanese word kyojitsu. Kyo means "void," and jitsu refers to one's actual ability. In one's mind, kyo and jitsu always appear and disappear. When any change in kyo and jitsu is perceived, one should strike a void (that is, a gap or weakness in your opponent's defenses) with one's full power, or jitsu. Proper timing is necessary to strike a void. The basic principle of tactics is to grasp a chance to mount an offensive through perceived changes in an adversary's kyo and jitsu.

PREPARATION FOR BATTLE

The body and the soul of a tactician must always be prepared for battle. If one is unprepared, one is certainly on the way to defeat. In a match, it is also important to speculate as to what techniques will be used by an opponent. One needs to carefully observe the movements of an adversary, find out his intention, and initiate a first strike to avoid defeat.

Victory in a match comes from a relaxed state of mind. To maintain calm judgment in a life-or-death situation, one needs a prepared mind. One will be able to act at will with a settled mind in a serious match if one is hard on one's body and mind in everyday training, prepares oneself for death, and immerses one's body and mind in tremendous fear. If one does not train seriously, one will be low-spirited and lack concentration in case of emergency.

Toku

GROUNDWORK FOR THE MIND

Creating solid ground on which the mind can rest is important in defeating one's opponents. If this is done, victory is almost always in one's hands. The following points should be kept in mind as one lays the groundwork:

* Think of opponents as merely a handful of dust, making light of them from the beginning.
* Grasp the opponent's real intention.
* Remove all fear and delusion.
* Elevate courage.

For one to be capable of rightly using techniques in a life-or-death battle, one needs courage to fight at the risk of one's life. The one who is more daring always wins in such a battle.

Force and Rhythm

Those who understand force can control others, and those who do not understand force are controlled by others. To defeat an opponent, one needs to understand and take control of the opponent's rhythm. Everything has its own rhythm, and one's life is no exception and can be exemplified by one's rise and fall. To avoid the fall, one needs to get the knack of rhythm of the fall. In a match, one should not fight with the same rhythm as one's adversary. Victory can be effortlessly obtained if one fights with a rhythm opposite to that of an adversary.

Mastering the right timing, which deflates the rhythm of an adversary, necessitates years of severe training. Such training will create eyes that can catch the movement of an enemy.

Mind, Intention, Wind, Water, and Ku (Heaven)

In a match, those who are less able cannot successfully use their techniques against those who are more capable (usually those of a higher rank). They will be controlled by them, will be unable to foresee their moves, and will be driven into a tight corner. A rank refers to one's overall ability, including sword techniques, sensitivity, and life experience. One's real rank cannot be exaggerated or feigned, and it is obviously revealed in a match.

The following are goals to strive for.

* **Rank of Mind**. Have an undisguised and immovable mind.
* **Rank of Intention**. Have selfless, unmixed, and clear intention.
* **Rank of Wind**. Have a clear mind and body like a wind when launching a first attack.
* **Rank of Water**. Flexibly react to the enemy's movements like water touching things.
* **Rank of Ku**. Be a sword stemming from the Heavens.

State of Mushin (Mindlessness)

A state of mushin refers to a mindless internal situation in which one observes and focuses one's concentration upon movements of one's adversary, and considers strategies to attack him or her. Mindlessness reveals the intents of an adversary. In other words, mushin is one's presence of mind. One's presence of mind, then, is courage. That is one of the qualities every tactician must possess. Without courage, mastered techniques cannot be utilized to the fullest.

The only way to diminish cowardice and cultivate courage is through training hard and the polishing of techniques. As one continues to training hard, one's mind unconsciously reaches a stable and unshakable condition. Lack of training will appear as disturbed courage at the time one stands up to face an adversary.

One's whole body should be kept free and relaxed. Such maintenance of the body requires the state of mindlessness, abandoning anxiety, fear, thoughts of the adversary's attack and defense, and all other considerations. Leaving behind things to consider, do, and desire, one should devote one's body and mind to the macrocosm. To one with a correct state of mind, one's adversary's intentions become quite clear and obvious. One can get one's hands on victory by securely seizing a chance to launch a blow.

Heroic Spirit
A hero is one who values honor, disregards life and death, and then practices the principles. He courageously does not submit to anything. There is nothing above or below him; he is all by himself. Those who use a sword need to acquire the spirit of a hero, disregard trivial matters, and take drastic measures.

MASTERY
Two factors determine whether or not one is able to master the secrets of tactics: boldness and cowardice. One must go through the process called *sanren* to reach the secrets. *Sanma* is to learn, train, and contrive as follows.

* *Learning.* Learning is trusting in all that one's instructor or predecessor says and endeavor to assimilate these lessons.
* *Training.* Training is a process by which one masters what is learned.
* *Contriving.* Contriving is to establish self-direction by surpassing training as originally taught.

To become a master, moreover, one must reach the state of *sanni ittai* (three principles in unification). Sanni ittai is to:

* Rightly follow teachings
* Have an undisturbed and tranquil mind
* Have *heijoushin,* or the presence of mind, which enables one to freely apply one's techniques

Heijoushin refers to the state where everything disappears from one's mind. This becomes possible by making one's mind void and clear like a mirror, abandoning the attached mind, and seeking the state of mindlessness by putting one's mind on a flowing, unwavering course. A master is an individual who does everything within this state of heijoushin. Lifelong training refers to the state of sanma and sanni ittai.

Shinmyouken

Shin refers to a mind, whereas myou is an expression of a mind—ken means a sword.

Man is by nature endowed with miraculous power. Spirit will never be aroused in one's mind if one's mind is not cultivated and trained. When one arouses one's spirit, one will be able to use miraculous techniques against one's adversary. Unless one has mind's eyes that instantly detect the ability of the adversary, one is less than perfect. When facing an adversary, one should always observe that person as he or she is. One should not be influenced by an adversary. Shinmyouken is the way to win by freely allowing an adversary to exercise techniques, and then rendering them ineffective.

Attitude in Using Techniques

Freely move along with the offensive movements of an adversary like flowing water. Do not stay in the same posture. One's mind should be clear and determined when executing techniques. Before entering the adversary's ma-ai (distance within which your opponent can strike you), settle your mind. Make your mind one that could catch a blowing wind and flowing water. This is the attitude one should have when executing techniques. Only with a strong spirit that transcends life and death, and a courageous mind, will one be able to effectively execute the techniques one has learned.

Breathing of a Tactician

Wrap your abdomen with a belt and tighten your abdominal muscles so as to confirm that power is felt in the abdomen. Those without power in the abdomen are not able to fell an adversary. Man's movement is slow while breathing in and fast while breathing out.

In a battle with its enemies, a beast takes a deep breath prior to approaching the target and keeps the breath in its chest while attacking. In the same way, a man's movement and breathing need to be in unison in order to thrust an attack home when the opportunity presents itself. At the moment one sees a chance, one should simultaneously have the feeling of attacking, setting one's body into motion.

The Way to Overcome a Desperate Situation

One should refrain from considering how to defend oneself from an overwhelming adversary. In such a situation, one should simply face the adversary from a state of selflessness.

If one has an undetermined mind, one will be dragged into the adversary's rhythm. To reverse this situation one must take the adversary into one's own rhythm, then, one needs to face him or her with a selfless mind. When one is in this state of selflessness, an adversary tends to believe that he or she can attack in any way, and is tempted to throw his or her best techniques. Under such a circumstance, without a moment's delay, one should evade the adversary's offensive and attack, thereby overcoming a desperate situation.

The Secret of Victory

Everybody has their own favorite moves: To attack, make a first move, defend, evade attacks, trap an adversary, or jump around in fighting. First, however, it is essential to recognize an adversary's favorite moves.

The secret of victory is to get an adversary off guard by letting the adversary throw his or her favorite techniques.

Sickness of a Tactician

A sickness of a tactician is the possession of a mind totally adherent to victory and attack or defense. Obsession with abandoning these symptoms of the sickness is also a sickness itself. In tactics, a sickness of mind refers to a situation in which a mind becomes totally rigid, adhering to one particular thought or movement.

Executing techniques with utter confidence and without thought removes the sickness. On the other hand, however, it is not a sickness to believe that an appropriate use of techniques will lead to victory without fail. The genuine effectiveness of any perfect technique cannot be delivered if one has a feeling of doubt in his or her mind.

Four Precautions

The words of those who have conspiratorial thoughts are reflected in their hesitant tone of speech. Their breathing tends to be in disorder, no matter how eloquent they are. The speech of a liar trying to deceive others is hesitant in one way or another. One needs to be cautious when faced with an adversary who is concentrating upon one particular thing. One who tries to draw near you or seeks to pull out his sword tends to glance at his opponent's sword at various times.

Never underestimate an adversary. One could lose one's life if one despises an adversary as unwise and stupid.

There are four precautions one should take when dealing with others:

* Listen carefully.
* Close your eyes and think creatively.
* Open your eyes wide and observe things thoroughly.
* Make guesses prudently.

The Way to Evaluate the Ability of an Adversary

One can estimate the ability of adversary by momentarily touching his sword at the instant that one reaches attacking distance, or ma-ai. Then, if the adversary flexibly fends off one's sword, it is almost certain that the adversary is skillful. If, on the other hand, the adversary stands still like a stone, one can easily claim a victory just by incessantly attacking the adversary. In a fight with swords, the one who has a bolder mind will handle the sword easily as his mind commands it, leading to victory.

How to Fight with Four Enemies at the Same Time

If one has enemies on one's left and right sides, first aggressively attack one side, turn around, and then attack the other side. If one takes proper steps to meet a situation like this, one can deal with large numbers of enemies at the same time.

Solitary Training at Night

Around 10 o'clock at night, start a solitary training session in a quiet place like a forest. First sit down, meditate to reach a state of mindlessness and selflessness, and calmly breathe in and out. Obtain spiritual unification through breathing, according to the instructions that follow:

* First, deeply inhale through your nose and exhale through your mouth. Put your palm on the point between the chest and abdomen.
* When exhaling, tighten your muscles to the extent that you will eventually sweat.
* Begin natural breathing.

Finally, deeply inhale, and yell out "Aaaa" with your mouth wide open, while exhaling. Take three steps to breathe out, as if you were to bring your voice from the bottom of the abdomen. Continue this process.

At the beginning of meditation, one's mind tends to be distracted and feel languid. In such a case, set your mind free and concentration will naturally come. After meditating for some time, calmly breathe as if you have come out of a dream, and practice your techniques several hundred times. Once again, sit down, calmly breathe, and meditate. Then stand up and practice techniques again and again. Repeat this process until dawn.

When one just begins the night training, one tends to have a ghastly feeling. But if one endures such a feeling, one's guts will get accustomed to it and eventually appreciate its exquisiteness. One should try to think of nothing at the onset, and when distracted, stand up and repeat one's techniques for five hundred, or even one thousand, repetitions. Then return to meditation once again.

✳ BOOK TWO ✳

LEADERSHIP

PEOPLE WITH OPEN and noble minds are the most effective teachers. Those who teach must not be bound by a single doctrine of existence—or an absolute value system. Regardless of their level of knowledge, their guidance cannot be fully effective unless they have a selfless mind.

Leaders should also be patient and kind, and teach fairly and with great mercy to all the people. They should have a great sense of responsibility, and their respectable behavior should give the people they're teaching a sense of well-being and peace of mind.

It is far more difficult to overcome one's own falsehoods and self-deception than to defeat millions of enemies. Unless you overcome these difficulties, however, you cannot preach morality. Self-centered thoughts and desires will eventually destroy your self.

If you are to lead, you must first lay your own foundation. Creating such a foundation will give others a sense of relief. They will then live rightly in the way that created such relief.

Similarly, a good partner relieves fatigue and arouses courage. It's a rare person who pays attention to their partner's strong points, corrects his or her direction if it's wrong, and furthers his or her abilities. But a wise person sees the joy in spending their life following and being dominated by a loved one. They can maintain a positive influence on the loved one, influencing him or her to make the right decisions at critical turning points in life. This is a good partner. In other words, a good partner is both a good leader and a good follower.

HAGAKURE

Secret Teachings

Lectures by Tsunetomo Yamamoto
Recorded by Tsuramoto Tashiro

"One should make a decision before the passing of seven breaths."

HAGAKURE CONCERNS the teachings of Bushido (The Way of the Warrior), handed down in the Saga Clan and secretly copied through the ages. This book contains the lectures of Mr. Tsunetomo Yamamoto (1659–1719), the retired leader of the Saga-Nabeshima Clan, which were delivered over a period of seven years and recorded and compiled by a younger member of the same clan, Mr. Tsuramoto Tashiro (1678–1748). This long work covers eleven volumes, containing a total of 1,343 chapters, and was written 100 years after the Tokugawa government had come to power; a time when peace was settling over the country. Stressing the need for discipline and reminding the people of the harshness of life, Yamamoto emphasized things that were beginning to be forgotten.

While the first chapter of his writing contains discussions of principles of one-to-one combat fighting techniques, Hagakure also taught about worldly wisdom and leadership. His writings not only stressed cultivation of moral character, but also taught practical wisdom that any person could follow to promote the welfare of his or her group.

Hagakure

THE FUNDAMENTAL PRINCIPLES
OF AN ORGANIZED BODY

In order for any organization or group to be founded, the historical circumstances and the vision and efforts of the founders are important. However, as the organization becomes stable, some will forget the principles of its founding and secretly begin to create trouble. Of course, the nature of the founding principles must change according to the demands of the time, but these changes should occur as a continuing process of evolution. An organization that forgets its founding principles, although it may appear to be well organized, will eventually disintegrate and collapse; one must not overlook the successive stages of the organization's development in the past.

DO NOT FORGET YOUR CIRCUMSTANCES

Since Buddha, Confucius, Kusunoki, Masashige, Takeda, and Shingen did not serve the Nabeshima Clan their words were considered unreliable (in the context of that clan). No matter how great the theory or principles may seem, if the circumstances and conditions to which they are being applied are ignored, then problems will arise and they are worthless. Consequently, as a prerequisite one should examine carefully one's own circumstances.

HAVE HIGH ASPIRATIONS
AND HOLD FAST TO THEM

The warriors of Nabeshima need neither strength nor intelligence; all they need is to be steadfast in their allegiance to the house of Nabeshima. As human beings, no one is inferior and, unless one has immense pride in oneself when undergoing training, all is naught. While training, one should think that one is solely responsible for the welfare of the house; unless it is undertaken with such a fervor, training will not bear fruit.

THE ESSENCE OF BUSHIDO IS GRASPED
WHEN ONE HAS ACCEPTED DEATH

When one has to choose between life and death, the only choice is death, which is not particularly difficult because one only has to be prepared for it. In Bushido, it is said that, "An honorable death is to have died for a cause even if one's goals have not been achieved." When a person has chosen to die for a cause, it doesn't necessarily mean that his judgment was correct. Most people rationalize their choice, since they would rather choose life over death. If one's judgment on a matter is proven to be erroneous, then one has to bear the shame of being called a fool. After one has died for a cause, even if one's judgment of the situation was wrong, whether one's death is hailed as an honorable or insane death is inconsequential. Such should be the attitude of the followers of Bushido.

An earnest follower must constantly, day and night, discipline himself to rid himself of his attachment to life. Only in this way can he become a true warrior.

The saying, "An honorable death is to have died for a cause even if one's goals have not been achieved" is the most famous in the entire book and was the slogan for the young men who fought in World War II. It is of great importance to reflect upon our present values and compare them with this terse expression of values held by the warriors of the past. In any era, accepting that statement as true is a great deed. Is not our present unhappiness due to an inability to have concrete goals and ideals for which we are willing to sacrifice our lives?

HOW TO SUGGEST AN IDEA

People often presume that complicated matters can be resolved only by thinking deeply about them but, no matter how deeply one thinks about things, decisions based on selfish interests and a subjective point of view will be erroneous. To remove self-interest in decision-making is most difficult; however, tragic mistakes can be avoided if matters are viewed objectively. To eliminate self-interest, learn what men of the past have said and seek the opinion of a neutral party. The person who can listen to the advice of others and counsel others, surpasses those who counsel or criticize him.

HOW TO PERSUADE

When speaking to a person, immediately determine his nature and act accordingly. To those who are argumentative and strong-willed, appear to be giving in so as not to create problems. After having won or lost an argument, hold no grudges. When persuading, do not create enemies, but increase the number of people who are sympathetic to your views. As a last resort, try to have an opponent take a neutral stand.

HAVE STRONG DETERMINATION

There is a saying that, "One should make a decision before the passing of seven breaths." To decide but to fail to carry out the decision is unwise; seven times out of ten this is just what happens, and then the decision itself will be questioned. It can be more effective to concentrate one's thinking into a short time.

WHEN CRITICIZING SOMEONE

To be open to criticism and to correct one's faults is to possess great character. This is a most important thing, although the process can be painful. Telling a person his strong and weak points is relatively simple. Most people know it is kind to tell others what they usually do not want to hear, and that which is difficult to say. If the person who is told refuses to listen, it cannot be helped, but it is a disadvantage to have such a narrow attitude. The person who tried to help is embarrassed, ill is spoken of him, and he is considered a fool.

When expressing an opinion, first determine if that person is willing to listen. Then, become such good friends that you can confide in him. The other person must have confidence in you. This can be fostered by discussing common interests. At an appropriate time and in the right manner, indirectly criticize him through letters or by speaking about these faults as if they were your own. Also, begin by praising him, so as to flatter him a bit. When he has had just about enough, express your point quickly so that he will accept it naturally. This is the best way to express one's opinion.

It is a difficult task since everyone has deficiencies and weaknesses that are so ingrained that correcting them is difficult. When peers can know each other well enough to give constructive criticism, then everyone will become one and truly there will be great compassion. How can one achieve one's goals by intentionally causing embarrassment?

HOW TO ACCEPT AN INVITATION

In accepting an invitation, find out about the other person and think ahead about the words of greeting and the contents of the impending conversation. It is proper etiquette to think beforehand about the other person so as to avoid embarrassment. This is the way to maintain harmony.

When invited by a person of high status, you will not enjoy yourself if you feel uncomfortable and nervous. Think positively by being thankful, and make it a point to enjoy yourself. If you have no reason to be there, then it is better not to be there at all. Unless you know how to conduct yourself, you cannot say you were a proper guest.

When you are invited, think about the role of the guest by realizing what kind of a situation it will be. Know how to drink on such occasions, as well as how to time your departure, which should be neither hurried nor delayed. In ordinary situations, when served food, it is polite to refuse. Therefore, do so only once or twice, and then accept.

MANNER OF DRINKING LIQUOR AT PARTIES

After excessive drinking, there are many people who cannot remember what happened, which is a most distressing situation. Know what your limits are, and do not exceed them.

Even with care, there are times when one drinks excessively. When in a drinking situation, do not be careless; one must be prepared for the unexpected. Since a party is a public place, be careful not to make mistakes.

HOLDING HIGH POSITIONS

It is said that fish cannot live in clear water; when reeds grow, fish can hide among them and develop. If little things are overlooked, then those working below will be relieved. Prudence is necessary when talking about a person's conduct, for to find fault in someone about insignificant things will cause uneasy feelings. Among those who find faults, many have no basic philosophy or ideas of their own. Those who overlook small matters do so out of love for the masses and because they have confidence in their policies.

DUTY OF AN INSPECTOR

Unless an inspector is able to see the overall situation, he is ineffective. Only by listening carefully and knowing the merits and faults of the administration, the voice of the people, the miseries and joys of the masses, will he be able to perform his duty of planning effective policy. His primary duty is to examine critically the works of the leaders. Inspectors responsible for the investigation of criminals should do so with the intention of trying to help them. Inspectors who are lenient to the leaders and unfair to the common people are irresponsible.

DO NOT FORGET ONE'S PLACE OF BIRTH

To have been born in country-like and simple surroundings is an important treasure; to want to be like others is to imitate. When a person told a priest, "The doctrines of your faith are so strict that I dislike them," the priest replied, "Because of its strictness, I believe in them. If they were not so I would find another faith."

HOW TO BE AN EXAMPLE

In wanting to become an example, especially about manners, ask yourself who it is that has courage, who it is that speaks well, who it is that carries himself properly, who it is that has integrity, who it is that is able to make decisions. The ability to recognize the good points in others and incorporate them in oneself will make one an excellent example for others.

When learning any art, the tendency is to look for the weak rather than the strong points of the teacher; this is a fruitless endeavor. Since everyone has good points, concentrate on recognizing these; then everyone will be a good example. No one is perfectly beautiful or a genius at everything, but everyone has something from which others may learn.

THE REARING OF AN HEIR

It is difficult to raise a person to succeed oneself. Even today, old-fashioned executives who boastfully say, "You don't know what they'll do unless you keep your eyes on them," will not be able to create successors. Those who humble themselves and can think of the other's welfare are men of great character.

WHAT IS LOYALTY

Towards a master who is peaceful and quiet, loyalty is praising him so that his works will proceed smoothly as he gains self-confidence and takes more initiative. Towards a master who is stubborn and smart, it is treating him so that he will become more cautious and avoid doing anything reckless. Great loyalty is doing things in such a manner that the master will think to himself, "I wonder what he thinks about me." When the clan has no retainer who can serve this role for his master, but merely has retainers who flatter him, no matter how well the master may rule, his works will eventually be undermined due to arrogance.

NEVER FORGET TO PERSEVERE

Stagnation begins when one is relieved and satisfied with small achievements. This can be the beginning of one's downfall as a result of not reflecting because of overconfidence. Only those who continually reexamine themselves and correct their faults will grow.

HOW TO BECOME A MAN OF TALENT

No matter what it may be, when one loves what one is doing, then great things will happen. For instance, if one is interested in flowers, even if at one time one had no flowers, one will be able to grow many varieties, even unusual ones. The same is true in becoming a man of talent.

As with anything, talent must develop naturally or it is useless. Discovering the merits of subordinates and nurturing them is a way to develop their talents. Good workers will not develop under a leader who feels that those below him are all worthless. Like any precious new growth, they will only grow if they are nurtured and not mercilessly trampled upon.

WHEN IN DESPAIR DO NOT GIVE UP

The right man in the right place is indeed the ideal condition, but as a member of a group, the possibility of being placed in a position he does not like always exists. When placed in such a situation, whether one gives up one's aspirations or encounters new work as a challenge will determine the nature of one's character.

VITALITY

Although there may be exceptions, a person with vitality makes greater contributions; this is especially true of the young. In contrast, those who are said to be good-natured are too reserved and cannot accomplish great tasks. Before one is forty, one should be boisterous, but at the age of forty, one should become a man of discernment or one will be considered unreliable.

IT IS USELESS TO DEPEND ON THE GODS

If one relies on the gods, then one will not be able to take risks. Unless one has the spirit to say to oneself, "If the god who took the side of the enemy should come towards me, I will break him in two," then one will not be able to win.

POINTERS ABOUT VERBAL ARGUMENTS

When involved in verbal arguments, it is good to reply, "I will think about it and then answer." Even when stating an opinion, make allowance by saying, "I would like to think it over," and discuss what has happened with other people and seek their advice. Increase the number of people who will support you in order to isolate the other person. Practice beforehand what you will say, making sure to cover the important points. Also speak to the other person first, as it may sound like an excuse if spoken later. Having outwitted the other person, persuade him with caution and have him respect you.

PEOPLE IN UNFORTUNATE CIRCUMSTANCES
When placed in an adverse situation, never forget any favor that was bestowed upon you. When persuading a person, telling him how grateful you were of his past assistance is most effective.

SPEAKING ILL OF OTHERS
When people in an organization point out the faults of others, insecurity arises causing a strain to the unity of the group. If rumors should reach the public, then the organization itself can be adversely affected. In such a situation, state your opinion to the officers secretly. People who have taken advantage of such a situation by speaking of the defects of others in order to increase their reputation have always existed. However, this type of behavior only breeds antipathy, and that person will be shunned by colleagues and those below him; this will result in his downfall. Having noticed something among colleagues, tell it secretly, for this will better solidify the unity of the group.

TEIO-GAKU AND JYOGAN SEIYOU
A Study of Leadership and Politics

By Taisou

"The less visible a leader is, the better."

TEIO-GAKU IS A STUDY of political leadership attributed
to Taisou (Le Sei Min), who was known to be a good ruler in the
Tang dynasty (626–649 C.E.). It offers guidance for manag-
ing an existing social system. The book touches on the moral
principles necessary to be a top leader with a focus on the knowledge and morality necessary for political leadership.

Jyogan-Seiyou is a book on politics in the form of questions and answers. It was edited by the Chinese historian Go
Kyou around forty to fifty years after the death of Taisou. The
central points of the book discuss how a leader must keep an open
eye, respect all life, maintain his self-discipline and politeness,
and accept candid comments in a positive manner. Taisou had
retainers who spoke plainly to him. He listened and acted upon
their comments. It is considered that his willingness to listen
contributed in no small way to his becoming an enlightened
leader.

"Jyogan" is the name of the era during which Taisou reigned,
and "Seiyou" refers to the morals for reigning over a country.

Together, these two books consider "ideal politics." The principles they offer can apply to any trade today.

Teio Gaku

LEADERSHIP

Taisou once told his vassals about the preceding emperors: "Chou and Shin had similar characters at the beginning of their reigns. Chou did many good deeds and became a man of virtue. This explains the longevity of his dynasty that lasted for 800 long years. Shin, on the other hand, lived in the lap of luxury and treated his people harshly. As a result, his dynasty was overthrown in the second generation."

Even Taisou was not a born good leader. In the old times, no leader welcomed remonstrance more than Taisou of the Tang dynasty. His close advisors were exceptionally down to earth. Taisou willingly accepted their remonstrance and bore up under their criticisms, which made him a tough and strong-minded person.

No competent leader can achieve great things without capable military officers. On the other hand, even with capable military officers and advisors, one cannot accomplish great things unless one knows how to fully bring out their talent.

Like Taisou of the Tang dynasty, Kouso (reigned 206 B.C.E. to 195 B.C.E.) of the Han dynasty was also praised by the people as a wise leader. Kouso tells the reasons behind his victory over Kouu.

"Let me give you an account of three of my men. First, Chouryu was a calculating man and used adroit means to change the minds of the enemy. In this respect, his abilities were superior to mine. Second, Shoka, was ingenious in governing domestic affairs, bringing stability to people's lives and procuring military arms. Again, in this respect, his abilities were superior to mine. Last, Kanshin skillfully commanded and controlled an army of a million. When it came to winning victories, his skills were superior to mine."

These were three preeminent men, but it was I who controlled and knew how to make use of their abilities. This was the key in conquering the country."

AN IDEAL LEADER

The following story comes to mind as an example of an ideal leader. A long time ago, a renowned breeder of fighting cocks was asked by the king to train a cock.

After ten days the king asked, "Is the cock ready for fighting?" The breeder replied, "Not yet, Your Majesty. The cock is now bloodthirsty, and it's eagerly seeking for an opponent but it is not ready for a fight."

Ten days later, the king asked again but the breeder's reply was the same. "No, not yet, Your Majesty. Hearing or sensing the presence of another cock raises its fighting spirits and causes the cock to bristle. It is coming along, but it is not ready for a fight."

Another ten days went by, and the king asked the same question, but the breeder had the same answer, "No, not yet, Your Majesty. At the sight of another cock, it stares and gets enraged, but it is not ready to fight."

After another ten days, the anxious king questioned the breeder, but this time the farmer said, "Yes, it is ready, Your Majesty. This cock no longer gets distracted by another cock's provocation. The cock reminds me of a woodcarving. Toku (virtue) has settled within the cock. No other cock could ever win against it, and most likely other cocks will run away at its sight."

In this example toku is the possession of ability, skill, and a strategic mind. Toku is an important quality in a leader. It is a leader's toku that determines the success of a business. Toku has a silent power of persuasion. A trusted leader with toku needs very few words to run a business.

In China, a person in possession of toku was called kunnshi, a man of virtue.

Reasons for Lack of Recognition

A man called Shunnshi who lived in the Chou dynasty during the Age of Civil Wars once said:

* Lack of recognition by one's superiors means that the individual lacks effort.
* Lack of recognition in spite of great effort means that the individual shows no respect towards his superiors.
* Lack of recognition in spite of paying respect to one's superiors means the individual lacks sincerity.
* Lack of recognition in spite of one's sincerity is attributed to the ineffectiveness of the efforts.
* Lack of recognition in spite of effective efforts is attributed to a lack of toku. A person who lacks toku will not be rewarded regardless of hard work or high achievements.

A kunnshi must not do any of the above. Possession of toku is an important quality in a leader. A wise and reasonable person is unassuming and hides rather than flaunts his or her talents and wisdom. Those that flaunt their talents are those that lack wisdom and comprehension. Concealing one's wisdom is the true form of toku. Moreover, pure wisdom is not enough to be a good leader. A good leader must also possess a generous and empathetic mind, considering the needs and feelings of the people, otherwise he or she will not be accepted. One must also note, however, that excessive empathy could work against one's will.

Excessive empathy towards people makes it difficult for a leader to act and make decisions, hence courage and decisiveness are necessary to avoid this situation. Decisions should be complete and practical. Ideally, one should be empathetic yet decisive. Lao-Tse, a philosopher in the Chou dynasty said:

Since he does not show he is absolutely right, people accept him even more.

Since he does not show off, people bring out the best in him.

Since he does not boast his achievements, people praise him even more.

Since he does not brag about his abilities, people respect him even more.

A man of nobility does not contend with others. Therefore no one challenges such a man.

When a noble leader rules a nation, he will place himself under the people and treat them humbly with respect.

When assuming a leading role, he should be humble and never pose as a ruler.

For these reasons, people do not feel oppressed by him when he is placed at the top nor does he see the people as obstacles.

And the reason for his warm acceptance is due to his talents and modesty towards his achievements. Naturally, people start to gather around him and follow his leadership.

CLASSIFICATION OF A LEADER

* A first-rank leader does not justify nor promote his actions. No credit is taken for his achievements, and no trace is left of his actions. He pays meticulous attention to details yet shows no sign of his attentiveness. He maintains a calm outward demeanor in spite of turmoil below the surface, like a duck swimming in a lake. Above all, he has a clear view of the large picture and is able to foresee the consequences of his actions. These qualities make a first-rank leader.

* A second-rank leader is respected and loved by his subordinates.

* A third-rank leader is feared by his subordinates.

* A fourth-rank leader is looked down upon by his subordinates.

An ideal leader is a person who can bring out the talents in each of his men to complete a task without doing anything himself. He doesn't need to have a hand in each of their actions, as he can bring out the talents and abilities of all his subordinates. Things will not run smoothly if a leader completes all the tasks and exerts his abilities. An ideal leader has a good handle on his men and delegates with no words, while exerting a powerful presence. To reach this level of control, one must have jutsu (art). Jutsu is the ability to:

* Punish and praise others—holding on to authority tightly
* Correctly and critically evaluate other's work—sometimes severely
* Conceal likes and dislikes; once shown they give the enemy a chance for attack and lower one's status
* Test the reactions of one's subordinates by posing an unexpected question
* Test one's men by pretending to be ignorant or by lies and tricks

Jutsu is necessary to be a leader.

A leader must not assume high valuation for his hard work and achievements nor should he expect to be thanked. The less visible a leader is, the better. Three requirements of being a leader are:

* Be a man of few words.
* Be modest towards people.
* Be able to suppress emotions.

Moreover, it is essential that a leader have strong negotiating skills. A leader must hide his true intentions and predict his opponent's thoughts. Second, when the organization is faced with a crisis, a leader must remain unchanged and calmly deal with the situation. Restlessness permeates the organization if the leader shows facial expressions and attitudes that reflect uncertainty. In other words, boldness, prudence, and self-control are three requirements for a leader. A firm belief must be cultivated in order to withstand and overcome crisis. How is a firm belief cultivated?

* Do not be mislead by false information.

* Gain the ability to make a sound judgment.
* Believe that you are doing the right thing and have faith in yourself!
* Be kind and empathetic towards others, and let your good nature express itself.

A leader may lead a country to destruction if a reckless person whose intention it is to entrap him misleads him. To avoid this situation, a magnanimous mind prepared to forgive and accept is necessary. What is magnanimity?

* To forgive and not blame others for minor errors
* To overlook other's secrets
* To forget old wounds

By following these three teachings, one will not only improve one's own character, but one will earn no enmity from others.

People do not gather around those with narrow minds (who behave in a petty manner). Raising people's ethics and interests and bringing out the best of their capabilities are essential factors in survival in this day and age of confusion. Merits must be rewarded and crimes must be punished. A firm stance is needed, distinguishing between kindness and sternness. Without discipline, people become accustomed to things and start to be more lazy and dependent. At the state level, this may pose problems in the governance of the country. However, one must realize that discipline alone is not enough to lead and guide people. Kindness and empathy are also important qualities.

Qualities a Leader Must Possess
* A leader must be able to bring out loyalty and faithfulness from his followers.
* A leader must show no signs of weakness and be provident.
* A leader must be convincing. Followers must realize that once the leader is betrayed, they will be punished. For this, one needs the power of obedience through discipline.

Courage is also needed in a leader. There are two types of

courage, shin (advance) and tai (retreat). A leader must possess the courage to withdraw until called for. Courage comes in different forms. Courage to move forward kills and depletes the body, but courage to move backwards saves and rejuvenates. A person must consider withdrawing from the front line once he has risen to the top, in order to prevent regrets. Once power and status are obtained, giving them up is difficult and is somewhat against human nature. However, clinging to one's status may eventually lead to losing it. It is important to withdraw to retain the honor of previous achievements and reputation. Eliminating ambition and wealth from one's life means to throw away unnecessary habits. Although a leader is burdened with much responsibility and the need for self-sacrifice, once at the top, he could withdraw from the front line and enjoy a second life, thus paving the way for further growth.

FRAMEWORK OF GOVERNANCE

Governance of a nation and treatment of a patient are alike. When a patient is in recovery, extensive care is needed to ensure a full recovery. Likewise, when a nation is in recovery, careful attention is needed to ensure stability. Do not let your attention down or the nation may crash to the ground just when it is on the verge of recovery.

Essentials of a Kunshi: For Proper Governance of a Nation
* Fair governance and love for the people
* Proper etiquette and respect towards prominent people
* Promotion for the wise and talented

Some Rules for Governing a Nation
* Correct and improve your attitude.
* Respect those with wisdom and virtue.
* Respect your parents.
* Show respect towards ministers.
* Listen and cooperate with ministers to govern the country.
* Care for the people as if they were your own children.
* Promote the development of industry.
* Establish friendly relations with people abroad.
* Get to know representatives of other regions.

WHAT IS A MEIKUN (AN EXCEPTIONAL AND DISTINCTIVE RULER)?

A person in power must first and foremost ensure stability of the life of the people. In a country with a responsible ruler the people can have no complaints. However, those rulers that indulge in luxury at the expense of the overworked and the overtaxed are only consuming their own flesh! A ruler must be reasonable if he wishes peace and stability for all. The collapse of a country is caused by rulers that give in to their desires. Unless one is able to contain one's desire for delicacies, entertainment, and women, expenses will be endless. Lack of dedication towards governing the country only leads the people into despair. Furthermore, if a ruler were to be impervious to reason, people would grow apart, they would criticize him openly, and some might even plan to revolt against him. Therefore, a ruler must not give in to desires nor lead an extravagant life. He must always be in the right, and his lifestyle must be a model for the people. He must also listen and incorporate the opinions of his allegiants.

The Difference between Meikun and Ankun

Meikun. A man of sagacity—a "bright monarch"

Ankun. A man who lacks intelligence—a "dark monarch"

Meikun was a ruler who listened to the voices of people around him. Meikun had his doors open for those who brought him wisdom and toku, and he incorporated their suggestions in the governance of the country. Since he listened and incorporated their opinions, he was accepted by all and was never attacked nor deceived by those with shrewd intentions.

A ruler has absolute power. Many have misused this power, which can lead to self-destruction. To avoid such an occurrence, a ruler must possess self-control and close confidants who would make up for his faults. To gain reliable confidants, a ruler must have the ability to foresee talent. A confidant must be someone who can be trusted, depended on, and consulted frankly. The choice of a confidant has a great influence on the fate of the ruler.

Ankun was a ruler who only listened to a selected few. He did not realize the severity of the crisis he was in until the people completely grew apart. Even after being surrounded by enemies, he still did not face reality. Not realizing that his towns and villages were devastated by rebels, he ended up ruining himself.

Ryoujin and Chuujin

Ryoujin is someone who assists the ruler in gaining the respect of a meikun. He is praised by the people and for generations his descendants thrive to keep the tradition in the family. Chuujin is someone who is either killed for his wrongdoings or for leading the country to atrocious destruction.

An Allegiant Is to a Ruler What Water Is to Fish

Lawful governance of a country is not possible if a Meikun hires notorious allegiants. The relationship of a ruler to his allegiants is like that of water to fish. Peace is maintained when both sides are in harmony.

The quality of a meikun, whether good or bad, is determined by his decisiveness. When pressed to make a decision, the outcome must be appropriate for the time. Of course to make the right decision, plenty of research must be done beforehand. It is important to be open to the opinions of one's allegiants and not be influenced by preconceptions. Accepting advice as well as not rejecting it is important. Listen to advice and the country will run smoothly and peacefully. Reject it and the country will be in a great state of disorder.

Chisha (and Meichi)

Those who can understand others have qualities to be a chisha. Those who understand themselves are real meichi. Understanding others is difficult, much less understanding oneself. It is virtually an impossible task. People who lack intelligence tend to boast of their talents and overestimate their abilities.

Sustaining a country is difficult. During a crisis, dependence on preeminent allegiants is prevalent; however, once the country overcomes the crisis and enters a stable era, it is easy to be careless. The allegiants also begin to think only of themselves. They do not try to support or correct the ruler's wrongdoings. The momentum diminishes, and eventually this leads the country to destruction. It is important that the ruler, at all times, has his act together for the daily governance of the country. He must always be prepared for the worst and have a countermeasure to ensure the security of the nation.

"Take Care of the Pennies and the Dollars Will Take Care of Themselves"

While attending to government affairs, there are times when one notices violations of the law. Overlooking such incidences and writing them off as trifles only leads to bigger problems. It is too late to rectify the situation once the problem reaches serious proportions. Ironically, all state-level crises are caused by overlooking these trifles.

There are two kinds of trifles: One is a mere trifle. The other is the kind that when left unattended may have a negative effect on the whole system or organization. It is important to differentiate between the two.

Why do people keep their silence? Reasons vary between people. A weak-willed person is not able to express his thoughts. Out of fear or lacking trust, those that have not served under a ruler do not express themselves to him. Out of fear of losing their ranks, those that cling to their positions do not enthusiastically express themselves. They have all reduced themselves to be "yes-men." For an allegiant to rectify the ruler's mistakes requires the courage and determination to risk his life. This determination is equivalent to that needed when storming into an enemy's territory.

HOW TO JUDGE PEOPLE

Observe the following points when judging a person:

* Who was intimate with him in times of difficulty?
* Who did he give to when he was wealthy?
* Who did he promote when we was in power?
* Did he do wrong when he was placed in a difficult position?
* Did he lose himself in temptation when he was poor?

Standards for selecting personnel during peaceful times differ from those used in times of war such as in the Age of Civil War. It is difficult to keep a balance between competence and character. In times of peace, one would choose character over competence.

The Essence of Employment

A well-paid job is always lucrative. However, it is not enough for an employee to provide material guarantees.

* Those who yell and reprimand will only have underworkers.
* Those who only give orders will have petty workers.
* Those who treat others equally will only have workers that are much the same as them.
* Those who show respect and listen to others' views will have workers that are ten times superior to them.
* Those that treat others with utmost courtesy and have a humble attitude towards learning will have workers that are a hundred times superior to them.

LOVE AND REASON

As birds abound in a dense forest and fish live aplenty in wide rivers, with plenty of love and reason in governing a country, people will naturally come together. All the disasters in life come from lack of love and reason. One must be on the alert, otherwise one forgets to practice love and reason. Do not forget this even for a moment.

Shikou (Supreme Fairness)

Men known as shikou were fair, compassionate, and unselfish. A ruler (kunnshi) should not behave selfishly, as the country is a public institution. Status and position should not influence attitudes and decisions, even if the person happens to be a close friend. Hiring capable men will lead to stabilizing the lives of the people. When hiring, judge a person by his talent and not experience. Even if the person happens to be an acquaintance, do not hire an incapable individual simply because of his experience.

One condition for becoming a leader is to be able to make the distinction between public and personal affairs. If one gives special attention to family or specific interest groups, employees may notice the unfair treatment and lose the motivation to work. Eventually this situation may lead to internal conflicts within an organization. Old people used to say, "It does not matter whether a man is a kin or an enemy, talented individuals must all be recommended for promotion to higher positions."

Modesty (To Be Honest and Humble)

A tenshi (emperor) must always fear the mighty powers of heaven, listen to criticisms from ministers, and never forget to be humble. Once a ruler begins to act humbly and ceases to show off, no one will challenge his talents, abilities, or decisions. Daily reflection on decisions made pertaining to the governance of a country is important and must not be forgotten, as it is the key to longevity of a country and salvation from the misery of defeat.

WORDS

Communication is difficult. Words from a ruler are extremely important and influential. One offensive word is enough to leave a permanent scar that may become a seed for revenge. Hence, a ruler must always be careful what he says in front of his ministers. Unlike the case of an ordinary person, even the slightest slip of the tongue made by a ruler can have detrimental consequences.

EDUCATION

Uneducated people involved in politics cannot make effective and rightful policies. An ideal leader must possess sound and comprehensive judgment. He must aim to become a well-rounded person.

The following are the qualities needed to become a leader, followed by their relative importance:

Transferable skills 25%
Innovation and Creativity 25%
Education and Culture 50%

GREED

Greedy people do not know the value of money. A ruler with greed will lead the country to its downfall. A minister with greed will bring himself down. Happiness and unhappiness alike do not walk in the door; people bring them in. Unhappiness is brought upon oneself through greed for wealth. Those who accept bribery only seek immediate gain and do not see the long-term consequences such as losing their job. There is little to gain and lots to lose.

LAW

The dead can never be revived. Thus, laws should be lenient. The laws and regulations of a country should be clear and concise, and once established they should not be easily changed. When making laws, facts must be investigated thoroughly and caution must be taken to prevent omissions.

TROOPS

Looking back in history, those who irresponsibly sent troops to combats for no reason have been defeated. Armaments are a country's weapons. Constant engagement in war can wear out the people of even the world's largest nations. However, when a peaceful country lets down its guard, it becomes vulnerable to invasion. Wearing out the people leads the country to its downfall. There is a threat of invasion if the enemy holds the country in contempt.

HOW NOT TO BEHAVE

Men at the top lead solitary lives. A leader must bear great responsibilities. From ancient times, even the most accomplished rulers have been known to lose their way. An important quality of a ruler is to be able to look at oneself objectively. Compare yourself to historical kings, and learn through their mistakes how not to behave, and do your best not to repeat the same wrongs. Self-management is one of the prime requirements of a leader.

FOUR DEEDS THAT LEAD TO POLITICAL DISORDER

* Ruling with falsehood and lies—forgetting the truth and virtue and relying on limited abilities
* Forgetting public duties and responsibilities and pursuing personal interests and desires
* Lacking restraint and self-control.
* Being materialistic, extravagant, and conceited.

FOUR THINGS A RULER MUST NOT DO

* Be deceived by predictions, fortune-telling, and superstitions.
* Be engulfed by religion. Everyone has the freedom to believe in a religion. However, if a ruler begins to preach the reli-

gion, then he should be a religious figure or a missionary.
* Let family interests interfere with the governing of a nation or the management of a company.
* Overdo things and surpass precedents when planning events.

THE MOST DANGEROUS MEN

Dangerous men are slick and have an insight to a ruler's mind. Hence they can make wrongful suggestions and make them sound legitimate. Such people take advantage of the wise and play with emotions so that people will turn against each other. A person that can bring such calamities is truly a dangerous person.

ENDLESS UNNECESSITIES

A tenshi needs only a small space to rest his knees, not a palace. Likewise, one only requires enough food to fill the stomach, not a whole display of delicacies. What are extravagant feasts for? There is only so much a man can eat. These feasts are only good for observing others eating; nothing good comes out of them. Also, one only needs a small space, the size of a tatami mat, to live and sleep.

OMNIPOTENCE

A man of authority is often self-absorbed, in a state of omnipotence. When people obey his orders and do as he says, he gets a false sense of omnipotence. To our surprise, Taisou, the leader of the Tang dynasty, never showed this sense of omnipotence. He observed other leaders' mistakes and learned how not to behave. He tried to learn how to balance people's interest and political affairs.

BASIS OF STABILITY

A leader of a nation must attend to the development of the manufacturing sector for the expansion of the economy. As suggested by the saying, "fine manners need a full stomach," it is worthwhile to give to those who do not have. Less pressure and freer minds will allow people to have higher morals. Hence, it is important for a ruler not to expect too much and to give before taking. Approach and conduct everything with reason, and momentum will be achieved. Seize the day with a plan, and a favorable outcome should follow.

OPPRESSION

To suppress freedom of speech is like blocking the flow of a river. Eventually the force of the water will lead it to overflow and flood the surroundings, causing a large number of casualties. It is better to drain some water and guide it to a channel. Similarly, it is best not to suppress the voices of the people and instead listen attentively to their criticism, because it is one of the best cures.

There are two ways of approaching politics: the *soft* way and the *hard* way. It is almost impossible to make people obey orders using soft politics unless a leader is virtuous. Generally speaking, it is best to approach politics in the hard way. These two ways are like fire and water. Fire is frightening. People are afraid of fire, and they do not come close; thus not many die of fire. Water is weak. People are not afraid of water; thus more end up dying because of it.

Loosen the reigns of command and people will become impertinent. When that happens the reins must be tightened and strict measures must be taken. However, if the reins are too tight, people will not endure and the reins must be loosened again. In politics, one balances power by tightening and loosening the reins.

HOW TO EFFICIENTLY ACCOMPLISH GOALS

Those with power win. This is an invariable principle. It is also known that those who depend on power lose.

* How could one win without fighting?
* Must one fight a losing battle?

With these two questions in mind, how could one gain victory?

* Win by diplomatic negotiations.
* Work out a plot and win; do not fight using force, but use your mind.

By diplomatic means, one can plot a scheme to contain the enemy and destroy it from within. In this way, goals can be accomplished more efficiently without violence.

THE HIGHEST GOOD

The highest good is like water. Water nourishes and saves without asserting itself. It always flows in places men reject, from high to low. One's attitude towards war should be like the flow of water: Look for the enemy's weaknesses, not his strengths. Water has no shape. Like water, there are no unchangeable attitudes towards war.

By adjusting and varying strategies, depending on the enemy's moves, a troop can win a superb victory. For a good fight, one must spontaneously use intense power. In a fight for power, there is no superiority. An opponent who may seem superior always has his faults. With the right conditions, positions can be reversed. Consider the following precepts:

* Pretend you can't when you can.
* Pretend you don't need something when you do.
* Pretend to get away and come close.
* Beguile them into thinking they have the advantage.
* Confuse them, shake their ground, and knock them off with a single blow.
* Against strong opponents, step back and prepare well.
* Against powerful opponents, withdraw from the fight.
* Deliberately irritate an opponent and wear him or her out.
* Maintain a low profile, and throw the opponent off guard.
* Tire a well-rested opponent.
* When facing a united team, estrange them from each other.
* Attack their weak points, and do the unexpected.
* The key to victory is in knowing the opponent as well as one knows oneself.
* Study the strength of the opponent, fight if the odds are in your favor, but do not fight if there is no chance to win.
* Make sure to have the lead when fighting.
* Break up the opponent's army, and force them to be on the defensive.
* Concentrate on attacking their weak points.
* When on the defensive, keep a low profile, and wait until the enemy wears out.
* When on the offensive, attack the enemy as if it were the last chance.

* Against strong enemies, one must pretend to be overwhelmed by their ability and throw them off guard. Then, attack them when they least expect it.
* Keep a tight rein on the home troops, and make sure to keep the soldiers focused so that they may swiftly respond to the enemy's moves.

To

GICHOU

"In order to look at a person, one must look first at what that person has done."

GICHOU WAS THE prime minister of Tou no Taisou. Taisou was surrounded by two types of officials—those who established systems and order, such as Bougenrei, and those who maintained systems and order, such as Gichou. Taisou governed while listening to the advice from both parties.

This chapter presents Gichou's method for evaluating individuals, and includes excellent directions for effective leadership, including the selection and control of subordinates. It also suggests correct actions that will promote and empower all, and advises against others that, if not avoided, are likely to cause an organization to collapse from within.

Zen Aku

THE SIX RULES OF "ROKUSEI"

Rokusei, which literally translates as "six rights," is a ranking system for righteous officials, and describes six desirable and important attributes. The best leader will possess all six attributes.

Six Rightly Actions

"Choku Shin" (Honest Official) can admonish his master's mistakes without fawning or changing attitudes even when a nation is in a state of confusion.

"Tei Shin" (Virtuous Official) exercises moderation, obeys the law, observes moderation, and refuses a high salary. Also gives away gifts received from others and leads a frugal life.

"Chi Shin" (Wise Official) has good judgment and knows what leads to success and failure and hence can prevent mistakes beforehand. By removing the causes of failure, he does not cause any financial worries to his master.

"Chyuu Shin" (Faithful Official) wakes up early, goes to sleep late, and works very hard. He encourages the master to hire and promote able and wise men. By praising and preaching the respectable deeds of the ancestors, he stimulates and encourages his master.

"Ryou Shin" (Good Official) advises his master of proper etiquette and teaches him not to think of losses and gains when it comes to doing good deeds. Also proposes great plans. He can cultivate the master's good and reform the bad.

"Sei Shin" (Sacred Official) can anticipate happenings and danger, and quickly and swiftly act to elevate his master to a higher position.

THE SIX RULES OF "ROKUAKU"

Six evil actions

It is bad to abuse a high-paying official position and neglect one's official duties and only care for those that are close.

It is bad to always agree and praise. One should ascertain beforehand what the master likes and makes him feel good by doing and offering all he requires and wants, rather than enjoying with the master without thinking of the negative consequences that may follow.

It is bad to be malicious, yet pretend to be timid. Looking gentle and smooth-tongued, such an individual may be relentless towards others and most often envies and dislikes good and wise people. He speaks well of people he has recommended, emphasizing the good points and hiding the bad. On the other hand, he speaks badly of people he envies, overemphasizing the bad and hiding the good. He devotes his energies to avoiding punishment and avoiding obeying orders.

It is bad to keep one's mind occupied with self-assertion and concealing wrongdoings. Such an individual causes trouble both in his own home and in the Imperial Court, where the leader governs the country.

It is bad to use power for one's own benefit and set standards for one's personal convenience. Such an individual creates wealth through building a faction around himself. He disobeys orders as he pleases and improves his position.

It is bad to fawn and deceive a master with the sole purpose of doing bad. Such an individual will conspire with others to deceive the master and spread the master's vice throughout the country. These people invite the downfall of a country.

THE ASSESSMENT OF PEOPLE

* Observe how a man of high social standing appoints and promotes people to higher positions, and one can see the true measure of that man.
* Observe how a man of wealth makes and distributes his fortune.
* Observe what a man does during his spare time.
* Ask for opinions of those individuals who spend their time studying and learning.
* Observe what they learned and did not learn during their times of hardship.
* For those of low social standing, observe what they do and do not do.

Carefully observe the above and test their talents before deciding upon their appointment. Advise them to use their good points to make up for the bad, follow the six rules of rokusei, and correct faults using the six rules of rokuaku. This way, without strict discipline, an individual becomes self-motivated and makes an effort to better himself.

Next one must consider how to locate and recruit talented individuals. Since the old days, talented individuals have been found through scouting and selection examinations. In order to look at a person, one must look first at what that person has done. Taisou believed that it was best to have few public servants and establish a limit. He concurrently appointed talented individuals to double posts. When the number of talented men was short, Taisou preferred to have a few capable men, since he believed that that would be less detrimental.

BASICS OF RULING

Ten Correct Thoughts

* When you want something, practice self-control by telling yourself that you have enough.
* When you start a big business, think of the people first and that it is important to be able to stop if needed.
* When attempting a dangerous deed, do things in moderation, using self-control.
* If a desire to become full should arise, remember that an overflowing sea is always lower than the river that feeds it.
* When playing, try not to overdo it, and when hunting try to have an escape route.
* When laziness strikes, be careful if you start something and be prudent when you finish it.
* If you are worried about not knowing something, openly accept the advice of your subordinates.
* If you fear slander and lies, first you must correct yourself and remove evil.
* When giving things to others, do not let joy cloud your judgment and give the wrong thing.
* When giving a punishment, do not let your anger determine the degree of punishment.

Ten Bad Thoughts

A poor leader:

* Does not stop to think of the consequences when it comes to wanting something.
* Acts on inspiration when a plan comes to mind, without thinking of the employees.
* Loses track of his position when aiming for a position with a higher status.
* Forgets the limits and loses himself in play.
* Forgets to work hard and make sound decisions once he has failed in expanding the business.
* Starts things casually and right away loses interest, without seeing them through to the end.
* Does not pay attention to the frank opinions of his subordinates because he cannot see through flattery.
* Enjoys the bad-mouthing of people, without attempting to put an end to it.
* Recklessly does favors for people.
* Forgets his rational mind when it comes to punishing others and lets his anger get out of limits.

Nine Virtues

* Be generous and know how to behave.
* Be able to peacefully resolve disputes.
* Be honest and polite and do not be blunt and inconsiderate.
* Have the ability to control but be modest.
* Look quiet and self-effacing but be strong in the inside.
* Be honest, straightforward, and gentle.
* Be undemanding but firm.
* Be strong and fulfilled from within.
* Be tough, be courageous, and have a strong sense of justice.

Nine Vices

* Being fussy and having no modesty.
* Being too harsh in resolving disputes peacefully.
* Being irresponsible, hot tempered, arrogant, and inconsiderate.

* Bragging without being able to control it.
* Being violent yet timid in the inside.
* Being heartless, untruthful, and without compassion.
* Having the habit of interfering without looking at the overall picture.
* Being visibly weak and empty within.
* Being timid yet secretive, doing wrong behind one's back.

A leader must correct himself using the ten rules of correct thought and preach to his subordinates to follow and expand horizons using the nine virtues as described above. A leader must also make sure that the right man is in the right place. Everyone can fully display talent if their faults are corrected following the advice of good and rightful people.

A leader of the Tei dynasty knew very well that good is good, nevertheless he did not attempt to use good men. Also he knew that bad is bad, but did not attempt to remove the bad. That led to his downfall.

An organization or system will cease to function if the ten correct thoughts and nine virtues described above are neglected. Remember them in your heart, and do not forget them.

SAI-KON-TAN

"Do not abandon everlasting values in pursuit of short-lived values."

SAI-KON-TAN IS A collection of essays by Kou Ji Sei (1573–1619), a citizen of the Ming dynasty. He wrote under the pen name of Kanshodojin, and his true first name was Oumei; however, other things about him remain a mystery. The work arose at a time when the long-standing Ming dynasty was plagued by problems that had developed over time, resulting in the gradual sapping of the system's vitality—similar to the gradual declines that have affected governments and societies throughout history.

One fascinating aspect of Sai-Kon-Tan is its depiction of the flexible characteristic of human nature—although we try to be honest with ourselves at all times, sometimes we face reality, and sometimes we try to escape from it.

Man's relationship to society is an important element in Kou Ji Sei's teaching. Man cannot exist outside his society. Even when one gives up all hope, one has no choice but to live among others. Man has only two choices: One is to seek stability of the mind by fleeing to the world of idealism. The other is to try to change the society along with those sharing the same ambitions. The work also addresses how to avoid becoming bogged down in worldly details. It advocates limiting one's desires and spending a fruitful life in a materially simple environment.

The work consists of two parts. The first part of the book explains the attitudes necessary for living in society. The second discusses the pleasure of getting away from the working world and interacting with nature. This chapter summarizes Kou Ji Sei's thoughts, showing the delicate balance between these two endeavors. Each person, when first born, is at one with nature. This quality is lost during one's lifetime, and only enlightenment restores this balance with nature. These writings underscore that true enlightenment brings one back to the simplest of matters, and leaves the enlightened individual at one with nature.

Sai

HOW TO REACH AN IDEAL STATE OF MIND

In a working world, an ideal state of mind is reached with one's free mind, regardless of one's kind of job or style of living. When you are puzzled by external appearances, it is because your mind is at a loss. If the independence of your mind is established, then even the working world will become the world of truth. If that is not the case, becoming a monk would not at all differentiate one from ordinary people. A man can achieve a tranquil heart by abandoning desires and greed. You do not have to pessimistically view the world as one filled with anguish. If you achieve a serene mind, you will not be bothered by sensations of the world and will not need to escape to a quiet place.

It is especially important for those with wealth and high social standing to have empathy for the poor. If you take advantage of being young and indulge yourself in recreational activities, you will at some time realize that the end of life is around the corner, but you cannot start your life all over again. When in your prime with youthful vigor, you should think about the misery that you will experience when you become old. To have a beautiful end of your life without being exposed to the sorrow of the aged, you need to keep a youthful spirit. This means that you must summon up your spirit and have a strong will to live to the very end, beautifully decorating the end of life.

You should show clemency for mistakes of others as much as possible. Although you may question people about their mistakes, you should never go too far. On the contrary, you should always question yourself so hard that it may seem excessive; self-growth will never happen without it. If you reflect well upon your past conduct, this will help you grow. When you help someone, you should not allow the act to linger in your mind and expect any return from him. When you trouble someone, you should always remember it, and never repeat the same mistake. While it is desirable to completely discard a grudge against others, you should never forget favors from others.

HOW BEST TO INTERPRET
COMPLIMENTS AND PRAISE

When you have high social standing, you are inclined to wrongly believe you are highly respected by the people. The fact is, however, that people merely pay their respect to your title or position. When in a low position, people belittle you just because of your low title. Since people respect your title, it is absurd to congratulate yourself on having a high title. If you believe people belittle you because of your low social standing and not because of your character, you have no reason to become angry.

Dilemmas and predicaments strengthen the mind and body to make you a better person. If you live through these difficulties well, you will have a tough mind and body. On the other hand, those who do not experience such circumstances will be weak and will not be helpful when the occasion demands.

You feel great when you receive flattery. It will, however, put you in danger as if you immersed yourself in a poison. Nobody feels good when given a bitter pill or candid advice. It will, however, create a foundation to improve your character.

KEEP A WATCHFUL EYE
DURING GOOD AND BAD TIMES

When things are going well, it is not excessive to say that everything ahead of you is harmful. When things are going well, you need to act carefully or you will dig your own grave. On the other hand, when in difficult times, it is as if you were surrounded by medicines and instruments to cure your disease. In such times, your ambition should become higher and your behavior more respectable.

When you cannot move things in a desired direction or you get sick of it, you should think about people suffering in much worse circumstances. When you feel as if you no longer care about anything, you should know that there are people who make efforts while steadily enduring their hardships. When things go smoothly, brace yourself and do your job. When things go wrong, do not despair. Genuine success can only be achieved by making full use of precious experiences called failures. It takes unwavering determination to withstand predicaments and continuously make progress.

Fame and wealth lose their values as times change. No matter how successful your business is, or how educated you are, it shall all disappear with death. You should not abandon everlasting values in pursuit of short-lived values. What is everlasting value? It is the value of a man. It vividly lasts forever, as the spirit of man is sublime.

A chance to make a comeback comes from the nadir of adversity. A sign of downfall already exists at the apex of prosperity and wealth.

Ai

CARVE YOUR OWN DESTINY

To successfully carve out your own destiny, you need a strong determination that would drive back even Heaven's will. If Heaven's will decides to give me less happiness, I shall make efforts to polish up my character and attain genuine happiness. If it decides to make me ill, I shall keep peace in my mind and make efforts to alleviate the pain. If it decides to give me hardships, I shall carry through my belief and overcome the hardships.

Ideals should be lofty, but they should not be out of touch with reality. Thoughts should be thorough, but you should not get stuck on details. Hobbies should be simple, but they should not be insipid. Needless to say, principles and opinions should be strict, but they should not be too radical. You should not accept favors just because you have had good news. You should not get drunk and grumble about daily discontentment. You should not totally abandon the work you have not finished just because you get sick and tired of it. You should not be nervous all the time, nor should you let circumstances take control of your destiny. Truth is found in the middle of these two extremes, or in the tactful spirit of flexibility. You should be prepared with flexible means.

Cultivation of your mind requires repetition over a long time as if you were forging metals. A mind cultivated in an easy way will be useless when the time comes. The door to your own future will not be opened without exerting effort. After such effort, it is important to develop a state of mind that holds the principle, "Do your best and leave the rest to Providence."

In an effort to raise your cultural level, you should have an attitude to outrun others. Otherwise, you will not become a man with a fine character. When you live in society, however, you need to have a mind of concession as if you proceeded one step behind others, or you will suffer from being unable to move forward just like a goat whose horns are stuck in a fence and which therefore cannot make a move.

Genuine happiness lives long only after you strengthen your mind and body by exposing yourself to both hardships and pleasure. Genuine knowledge comes only after you believe, speculate about, and vigorously think about a subject.

✳ BOOK THREE ✳

ENLIGHTENMENT

IN ORDER TO BE spiritually awakened one must train to understand the area of psychology; to discover the cause of phenomena which exists within the human mind. It is a way to pursue infinite truth. To seek infinite truth is to obtain the means to control one's life. It is training to realize what our ancestors have accomplished in their own spiritual awakening.

Personality can deeply affect one's training. Personality can be categorized into two types—either thoughtful or intuitive. A thoughtful personality finds importance in practicality, practice, and observation. An intuitive personality finds importance in inspiration, imagination, and theory.

In order to be spiritually awakened, one must strike a balance between these two personality types.

TEN LEVELS OF ENLIGHTENMENT

By Kok Yim Ci Yuen

ABOUT 900 YEARS AGO in Sheung Tak Fu, China, the Buddhist sage Kok Yim Ci Yuen was saddened that the world had fallen away from spiritual enlightenment, and had become mired in the physical world. This sage was the twelfth or thirteenth in succession from Shaka Buddha (the founder of Buddhism). Kok Yim Ci Yuen hoped to restore true happiness to people by helping them to develop their spiritual selves. He realized that all people are born with complete freedom from worldly trappings, but that their spiritual mind becomes clouded during life. Recognizing the tremendous difficulty that the average person has in embracing spiritual precepts, he presented the following beautiful and insightful story as a guide, to allow one to measure progress along one's way to spiritual enlightenment.

Kok Yim Ci Yuen describes the stages of spiritual development by telling a story of a boy who takes on the task of finding and training a cow, which he considers to be the potential source of his enlightenment. Much like the parables of Jesus, this story was intended to be understood at some level by all who heard it, that, over time, they might find deeper and deeper meaning within it.

Interestingly, in terms of martial arts practice, these stages actually describe the level of enlightenment that accompanies achieving each of the ten Dan levels (ten levels of black belt).

Stage 1: A confused boy, in his search for the cow (which represents to him enlightenment), heads into the forest. He, of course, does not find the cow there and is consumed with worry. He is lost and needs guidance.

This corresponds to Shodan, where the new black belt has some technique and the knowledge that he must seek guidance, but cannot advance effectively on his own.

Stage 2: The boy searches diligently and finds a footprint! He is thrilled! He feels as if he has found a good textbook that he can study and gain knowledge from.

This stage corresponds to Nidan, second degree black belt, where the individual tries to attain further knowledge from any source, not necessarily the best source.

Stage 3: The boy finds the cow, but can only see half of the cow at any time.

This corresponds to Sandan, where the individual begins to understand nature, but can really comprehend only a portion of nature and life.

Stage 4: The boy catches the cow, and can see all of the cow. But he still has trouble, because he cannot control the cow. The cow refuses to obey him.

This corresponds to Yodan, where the individual feels at times as if he understands nature and himself, yet this understanding seems to slip through his fingers like smoke; he remains confused at times.

Stage 5: Here the boy begins to learn to control the cow. He cares for it and nourishes it.

This corresponds to Godan, master level, where the individual begins to comprehend truth. He still has much to learn, however.

Stage 6: Here the boy controls the cow completely—he can ride on the cow, and the cow will do his bidding. He relaxes completely and plays the flute while riding, because he no longer even has to cling to the cow.

This stage corresponds to Rokudan, where one day feels like an entire lifetime. The individual can relax and live a natural life without worry, without thinking.

Stage 7: Something new occurs here. The boy is alone—he doesn't seek the cow. Up until now he considered the cow as his quest, his source of enlightenment. Now, he realizes that enlightenment and understanding are to be found within himself.

This stage corresponds to Shichidan, where the individual begins to find enlightenment within himself, where his body and mind meld into one, where true happiness comes to him naturally.

Stage 8: The boy has forgotten completely about the cow. In fact, he has in a way forgotten about everyone and everything. At this stage everything is one, all is equal, and nature is balanced to him.

This stage corresponds to Hachidan, where the individual's mind is never disturbed regardless of the circumstances.

Stage 9: Up until now (Stages 1–8), we have witnessed the boy working hard, training, learning, and preparing for practice of what is to come. Now, with this stage, we enter a new spiritual level, where the time for training has passed. Here the boy is pure, like a newborn, with no concerns, thoughts, worries, or distractions. He lives in a spiritual stage, and life feels perfect.

This stage corresponds to Kudan, where enlightenment and unenlightenment merely blend into a circle—he no longer even considers the need for enlightenment.

Stage 10: This final stage is where the boy uses his own enlightenment for the good of others. He lives much like a saint; he moves through a world that is purely spiritual, and he exists only to help others. In this image, the boy, having attained enlightenment, is represented as the old sage, who is helping yet another boy begin his own journey.

This stage corresponds to Judan, tenth degree black belt.

HARMONY

"When you are hasty, close your eyes and calm your mind."

MIND AND CONSCIOUSNESS

Our bodies were given to us by our parents. It is one's mind that controls one's body. At the center of our everlasting soul, there exists the mind. When one is awake, one believes that the physical body itself is oneself. However, this is not the case when one is asleep. One is actually self-aware only when awake. This self-awareness in fact extends beyond our physical bodies. Even the world can only exist with self-awareness. Self-awareness expands infinitely like the universe. This self-awareness is a mind reaching the mind of god; this is the unchanging soul.

Wisdom and Knowledge

Knowledge is something one learns in daily life. Wisdom is something immanent in living experiences. Wisdom does not come from knowledge or the workings of the brain. Nor does a brain full of knowledge bear wisdom. It is the subconscious awareness in one's mind that engenders a treasury of wisdom.

Virtue and Mind

Wisdom comes from a peaceful, pure mind. Virtue comes from goodness. With a pure mind and an attitude that takes delight in the truth, one will naturally come to be a person of virtue. No treasure is more worthy of our desire than virtue. In order to give others peace of mind, one must first be healthy in body and mind.

Modesty

Understanding oneself begins with a modest mind. One should recognize that now is the time to cultivate one's mind or the chance will never come again. One has a tendency to overestimate oneself. If such overestimation is based upon one's status, fame, or knowledge that one is in some way superior to others in some other way, it is difficult to understand oneself.

Compromise and Harmony

Those who have a sense of guilt, have an inferiority complex, or are vain do not have the courage to calmly recognize their faults and short-comings; they convince themselves that they are noble by speaking ill of others. People with courage distinguish what is right from what is wrong, and what is fact from what is not. They are intelligent, and have the ability to calmly criticize and judge.

A compromise is nothing but a temporary breakwater to prevent destruction. No sympathy is found in a compromise since ego is involved in it. On the other hand, harmony brings about infinite progress and peace of mind. There is love underlying harmony. Love is a great bridge leading to peace.

Mind and Harmony

What unsettles one's mind? Why does one grow excited? Where does irritation of one's mind come from? What is most important in harmonizing such a disturbed mind is correctly understanding what is right and wrong. More often than not, selfishness and egotism are the leading causes of a disturbed mind. Reflecting on what one has done allows one to know the real state of one's mind and realize how absurd it is to adhere to things. Understanding the true state of one's mind will slowly diminish discriminatory thought and reinforce egalitarianism. Taking one step forward, when consideration based upon experience takes root, will lead the mind of love to grow.

As the mind of love grows, one will no longer be angered by every inharmonious word and deed of others. When one no longer gets angry, one's mind will not be poisoned by anger, hatred, jealousy, or complaints. As one's mind becomes free of such poisons, others will come to be cheerful and listen to one's opinions and deeds. One should not let one's own convenience or ego take control of what one does. One should take care of things surely and steadily. This will foster continuous progress.

Courage, Effort, and Understanding

Understanding and good deeds change one's mind. Such change needs courage and effort. Courage refers to a mind that does not stand in awe of God's plans. Courageous people perform their duties without being distracted by current customs. A sense of courage will degenerate if one confines oneself to the thought of self-preservation. Degeneration will keep one away from great wisdom, courage, and God's reason.

What is effort? Effort acts like a fuse leading from knowledge to wisdom. Those who have courage and continuously put forth effort will discover great wisdom inherent in themselves and be able to spend their days harmoniously.

THE PURPOSE AND DUTY OF LIFE

Understanding the purpose and duty in one's life is difficult. Those who come to grasp their purpose and duty will spend their life filled with joy and appreciation for life; there will be no self-preserving drive, ego, artificial conflict, or destruction. Instead, peace of mind and eternal peace will be realized.

WHERE DOES SUFFERING COME FROM?

Suffering issues from three sources: greed, anger, and absurdity. These are called *sanku*, the three sufferings. Sanku can be prevented by admonition, mind, and wisdom. Admonition wipes out greed. A rightly harmonized mind takes away anger. Wisdom eliminates absurdity.

SANDOKU (THREE POISONS) OF MIND

Sandoku consists of grumbling, anger, and desire. Grumbling engenders self-denial and feelings of estrangement and solitude. Anger brings out destruction. Desire will result in the loss of self. One should understand that these poisonous elements are deeply rooted in the thought of self-preservation.

ACTION AND REACTION

When insulted, people are tempted to speak back or counterattack. When people try to represent their thoughts in their actions, reaction will always follow. A retaliatory thought is always accompanied by adversity. People should be wary of action and reaction.

ATTACHMENT AND FEAR

Fear comes from instinctive attachment. One can keep fear at bay only when one discards attachment and follows the laws of nature and God's plan. Fear can be overcome by deepening experience through self-examination and practice. This is not an easy task, but if one can remove oneself from attachment and fear of death, one will come to discipline oneself, and then realize that it is but oneself who is held in fear without delight. Attachment comes into one's mind. This then keeps one held in fear, since one is misled by the five senses and six roots of consciousness (eyes, ears, nose, tongue, body, and mind). One's life can and should be a delight in itself.

FOUR METHODS TO HELP CONTROL YOUR MIND

- * Relax your shoulders, and your mind will be settled.
- * When you are hasty, close your eyes and calm your mind.
- * When you are unable to make a decision, look up at the sky.
- * When sorrow overcomes you, stretch your back.

BREATHING EXERCISES TO PROMOTE HARMONY

The basis of life is breathing. In distressful situations, one should therefore simply return to breathing as a method of clarifying matters and restoring harmony. These exercises are appropriate for different situations, but each should be practiced for at least five minutes. One must always inhale down to the abdomen. In the last two exercises, where one is exhaling via the mouth, one should exhale longer than one inhales.

Energetic Breathing

This method helps you build up energy.

- * Breathe in and out to and from your abdomen, using only your nose.
- * At first breathe slowly.
- * After a few minutes, breathe faster and stronger, still using only your nose.

Relaxed Breathing

* Breathe in and out to and from your abdomen, inhaling slowly through your nose and exhaling even more slowly through your mouth.
* Swallow your saliva as necessary.
* Maintain slow, relaxed breathing, but concentrate on each phase of your breathing.

Meditation Breathing

* Breathe in and out to and from your abdomen, inhaling slowly through your nose and exhaling even more slowly through your mouth.
* As you inhale, feel as if you are drawing in the universe.
* Swallow your saliva as necessary.
* As you exhale, let yourself melt into the universe.

THE PURPOSE OF MEDITATION

The purpose of meditation rests upon reflection. Reflection makes up an indispensable element in meditation, which clears up one's mind and brings one to candidly acknowledge shortfalls, and repent attachment. Progress is derived from reflection. Reflection through meditation deepens and enriches one's mind.

GASSHOU AND PRAYER

People often join their hands together. Such an act is *gasshou*, which implies well-balanced harmony and a balanced course. Through gasshou, one vows to seek a well-balanced mind and life. Peace of mind results from a harmonized, balanced course of life and mind. It does not come from polarizing thoughts such as complaining, anger, and greed. Spending a life with a right mind, which does not deceive itself, is a matter of paramount importance.

What is prayer? True prayer is not to depend on somebody, even on God, but to harmonize one's mind to ensure right deeds and thoughts. It should be accompanied by an appreciative mind.

Gasshou

SATORI

*"With the image of a peach flower kept in the mind,
one is able to maintain tranquility."*

SATORI REFERS TO a state of higher awareness. It is a state of spiritual awakening, in which one can perceive all aspects of life with complete understanding and amazing clarity. Satori is achieved only when one has perfect control over one's state of mind. The following considerations describe steps that can help to promote a state of satori.

Satori

LIFE, DEATH, AND PEACE OF MIND

Life and death coexist. So do happiness and misfortune. One cannot eliminate one without losing the other. Understanding this is much like realizing that there can be no finish without a start, no up without a down, no back without a front. Those who seek after the truth must actually "rise above" life and death, which means not to cling or be "attached" to either life or death. This does not mean that one cannot or should not enjoy oneself. Exactly the opposite—one's life should be a joy in itself! This seems like a contradiction, but it is not. What is meant here is that a much deeper happiness and enjoyment of life are derived from tasting life fully yet not fearing death. Genuine freedom starts at the moment when one's mind relinquishes such clinging and attachments. A thirsty person cannot enjoy a drink if he spends the entire time worrying that the drink will not be enough. One similarly cannot fully appreciate one's life if one constantly fears death. Since one is alive, one will eventually die, and one must recognize that death is drawing closer day by day. A simple approach to promote peace in oneself, and to rise above fear of death, is not to waste time—treat a day as equivalent to a whole life.

THE WAY TO OBTAIN GENUINE FREEDOM

It is important to realize that genuine peace of mind exists within one's mind itself. In the midst of the balance of happiness and misfortune, one can devote one's efforts to good causes, which lead to desirable results. Developing a cycle of devotion to good causes and achieving desirable results, yet remaining unattached to the results, can promote genuine peace of mind. The greatest gratification is embodied in the knowledge on one's deathbed that one has no regrets from his or her life, and that one has spent one's days with a sincere and harmonious attitude.

MUJYOU (TRANSIENCE)

A beautiful flower brings consolation to one's eyes, but the flower will eventually fall. All phenomena caught by the eyes are nothing but an instant dream. By keeping the image of a peach flower in one's mind, one is able to maintain tranquility. Once again, one should not forget that one is getting closer to the end of life every second.

GRATIFICATION OF *SANMAI*
(TRANQUILITY AND PEACE OF MIND)

Death comes unexpectedly. Human life is fleeting. One should not put off until tomorrow what one can do today. One should organize one's mind and appreciate the end of another day. One's mind should not agonize over anything. This will ruin one's life. One's mistakes should be admitted and corrected. A life with no repetition of the same faults as in the past enriches one's mind, freeing oneself from a life otherwise filled with suffering. Without any attachment and with tranquility in mind, one can truly enjoy the gratification of *sanmai*.

HATSHO-DO (EIGHT PATHS TO RIGHTEOUSNESS)

Human beings are, of necessity, affected by the five sense organs (eyes, nose, ears, tongue, and skin). However, one's mind should not be influenced by the five sense organs. To avoid such influence, there exists Hatsho-do. Hatsho-do consists of eight criteria, all of which are intended to help one's mind transcend the five senses as follows:

* Look in a correct way. This means to look at things in an objective, rather than subjective, fashion.
* Think in a correct way. To think is to ponder. Think from the standpoint of a third person.
* Talk in a correct way. Words should be expressed with a pliable mind and with empathy.
* Work in a correct way. With gratification and a service-oriented mind, one should work to harmonize relationships with others. A place of work is where one's mind and soul are nurtured and enriched.
* Live in a correct way. One should develop one's strengths, correct one's weaknesses, and try to create a cheerful atmosphere. To correct weak points, one should examine one's mind from the viewpoint of a third person.
* Seek the truth in a correct way. One should try to create an environment and relations with others which lead to a long-lasting communal life. Regarding human relations, seek a mutually respectful attitude.

* Pray in the correct way. One should examine whether one's prayer is based upon acts of harmony and love.
* Follow the correct path in a correct way. One should live one's life based on correct, moral thoughts.

Michi

SIMPLE APPROACHES TO OVERCOME HARDSHIPS IN THE COURSE OF LIFE

Although much of what is written herein represents lifetime goals, some very simple steps can be used to begin to overcome hardships in the course of life. These include:

* Take control of observable, inharmonious phenomena.
* Do not be misled by what you hear.
* Suppress egoistic words.

BASIC PRECEPTS ON HOW TO LIVE LIFE

Nature tells us how to live a well-balanced life filled with love and harmony. A day begins. One starts a day with appreciation. One gets up in the morning and washes one's face. One works with gratitude and dedication in the afternoon. One rests at home at night and ends a day with thankfulness and reflection on what one has done. This is how to live in accordance with the laws of Mother Nature.

To live humanly means to train one's own mind. Constantly reflecting on what one has done is not desirable since it narrows one's mind. On the other hand, if one neglects to reflect on one's past deeds, one's ego comes in to govern one's life.

Working and resting when one is supposed to brings about a humane life—this is a difficult balance to achieve. Whether it is an individual, a group, or a society, loss of moderation, harmony, courage, equality, appreciation, reciprocity, and mercy will lead to desolation of one's domestic peace and society.

AN ENRICHED MIND

One who, regardless of one's property and social status, is satisfied with life, trusted by friends, takes good care of others, and enjoys mutual trust in his or her family has peace of mind. Such a person bears no discontent in life. This is the person with an enriched mind.

Sei Mei

LOVE

All human beings want to be loved. However, the only person who can truly cherish oneself is actually oneself. Happiness comes to those who can cherish themselves. Those who can love themselves well can also do the same for others. True love is when one loves others in the same manner as one loves oneself.

A MAN OF WISDOM

A man of wisdom is independent, with a free, enriched mind, who gives and shares happiness with others. He has a sense of solidarity, fulfills social duties, and leads people along a right path cheerfully and gently. A man of wisdom is the one who always has an attitude of appreciation and tries to express his kindness and gratitude to everybody. On the other hand, one who cannot appreciate what others have done for him is a man of folly.

A splendid life with peace of mind and harmony will be obtained after one abandons any attachments and focuses on a feeling of satisfaction. Those who lead a balanced life are hard on themselves and soft on others. They are able to open their mind's eyes, be blessed by the love of a god, and see beautiful Mother Nature and the heavens.

Kokoro

AFTERWORD

I hope you have noticed unifying principles and ideals expressed by the many masters from whom I have quoted. It is noteworthy that humankind throughout history has invoked many methods and pathways to enlightenment, yet there is only one essential truth that is sought after by all.

The same is apparent among the many styles of martial arts that have evolved over the centuries; they all seek the same place. Moreover, the so-called "hard" styles have softness within their core, and the "soft" styles invoke hardness within theirs, although such may not be apparent until one has practiced for a lifetime. Indeed, this can be likened to the many modern languages—some are harsh-sounding, some are soft, yet the same beautiful sentences, or the same hateful curses, can be expressed in all languages.

I hope that continued examination of the words of these masters will guide you in your progress towards enlightenment.

Yume

Shi Sei

ACKNOWLEDGMENTS

I dedicate these writings to my teacher, Professor Isao Obata, for his continued interest and encouragement.

I am especially grateful to the following individuals: Professor Isao Obata for his teachings and encouragement, my first teacher, Soke Tamotu Isamu, Mr. Keiichi Hasumi for his support and letter of recommendation.

Special thanks to the following individuals, presented in alphabetical order, who assisted to varying degrees in the generation and completion of this book: Tomomi Aozono, Miri Arai, Susan Mogari Catican, Charles J. Garzik, Yuka Cumming, Kyoji Kasao, Martin S. Katcoff, Arthur R. Kerr, II, Kanae Koh, Peter Marsh, Charles Meriwether, Hiroshi Minato, Sandy Rosner, Thomas B. Shea, Danny Silverio, Mr. and Mrs. Kazu Uji, Paget Wharton, Shinya Yamada, Tse-Hwan Yong.

The author also thanks the following for their help and inspiration over the years: John Almeida, James Ambrose, Jordan Berry, Ikuko Buruns, Cosmo Capobianco, Bill Charles, Debra and Stuart Chassen, Billy Conigliaro, David D'Amore, Sam DeMarco, Ted Fowler, Takeshi Fukunaga, Harold Gold, Dov Goldstein, Robert Gomes, Noritoshi Gondai, Robert Harb, Joe Hizni, C. J. Hunt, Maria Jose, George Kasaro, Misako Kinoshita, Sifu Kasao Kyogi, Joe Laquidara, Matthew Levin, Malte Loos, Debra Martina, Susan and Nagao Matsuyama, Bob McNeil, Popsi Narasimhan, George Noone, Bob Perrin, Eymard Riel, Gene Shendoc, Vernon Simons, Sachi Suzuki, Jim Tatoski, Beverly Thomas, Roger Trimm, Masami Tsuruoka, Kaede Uji, Lloyd Webb, Dwayne Williams, Curtis Wong, Gayle Yoshimoto, Michael Zebrowski.

REFERENCES AND ORIGINAL CITATIONS

Kamiko Tadashi. 1955. *Hagakure*. Tokuma Shoten.

Funakoshi Gichin. 1958. *Karate-Do-Kyohan*. Nichigetsu-sha.

Sato Kenji. 1962. *Sonshi No Kenkyu*. Kanazawa Bunko.

Kamiko Tadashi. 1963. *Gorin-sho: Miyamoto Musashi*. Tokumashoten.

Kamiko Tadashi, Yoshida Yutaka. 1965. *Sai-Kon-Tan*. Tokuma Shoten.

Akizuki Ryomin. 1967. *Suzuki Daisetsu No Kotobato Shisou*. Kodansha.

Kawa Osho, Yaku Osho. 1967. *Kiseki No Tankyu*. Sakushin Meisou Center.

Moriya Hiroshi. 1968. *Jogan Seiyo*. Tokuma Shoten.

Ikeda Satoshi. 1970. *Fudochi Shinmyo Roku*. Tokuma Shoten.

Kazumi Tabata. 1970. *Power Karate 1.2*. Bermuda Press.

O-Mori Sogen. 1970. *Yamaoka Tetshu*. Shunshu-sha.

Daidoji Yuzan, Toshida Tutata. 1971. *Budo Shoshin Sho*. Tokuma Shoten.

Takahashi Shinji. 1971. *Gensetsu Hannya Shingyo*. Sanpoh.

Matsubara Taido. 1972. *Hannya-Shingyo-Nyumon*. Shodensha.

Narise Norisoku. 1972. *Saimin Ryoho*. Bunko-Do.

Sato Koji. 1972. *Zen-Teki-Ryoho-Naikan-Ho*. Bunko-Do.

Akatsuka Yukio. 1974. *Kino Kōza*. Kodansha.

Wada Sadaharu, Nishitani Ken, Tamura Masataka, Kuwabara Koji.
　　　　1977. *Karate-Do-Nyumon*. Natsumesha.

Dendo-Kai. 1979. *Butkyo Dendo-Kai*. Dendo-Kai.

JICC. 1979. *Yumeno-Hon*. JICC.

Kazumi Tabata. 1982. *Amerika-Jinni-Kaibuto-Yobareta-Otoko*. Natsumesha.

Kazumi Tabata. 1983. *Karate-Jyu-Kumite*. Natsumesha.

Yamamoto Hichihei. 1983. *Teio-Gaku*. Nippon Keizai Shinbunsha.

Dione Fortune, Oonuma Tadahiro. 1985. *Shinbi No Kabara*. Kokushio
　　　　Kanko Kai.

Mano Koichi. 1986. *Karate Training Machine*. Fukusho-Do.

Nippon Seisho Kyokai. 1987. *Seisho*. Japan Bible Society.

Matsubara Taido. 1988. *Gintoku No Kenkyu*. Shodensha.

Kawasaki Nobusada. 1989. *Chibetto No Shisha No Sho*. Tokumashobo.

Nakumura Tenpu. 1990. *Seidai-Na-Jinsei*. Nippon Gourika Kyokai.

Takagi Fusajiro. 1991. *Karate Sensei No Hitorigoto*. Takagi Fusajiro.

Naito Takenobu. 1992. *Karate-Do Dokushu Kyohan*. Tokyo Shoten.

Katsuyuki Ogawa. 1993. *Seikaku Bunkai*. Kodansha.

Kasao Kyoji. 1994. *Chugokushi-Bujutsu-Taikan*. Fukusho-Do.

Paul Epstein. 1995. *Kabara No Sekai*. Seidosha.

William G. Gray, Taku Katsuhara, Kenji Tosho. 1996. *Kabara Majutsu No Jitsen*. Kankohai.

Zen-Nippon-Karate-Do-Renmei. 1996. *Karate Do Kyohan*. Zen-Nippon-Karate-Do-Renmei.

Fili. 1997. *Chakras Book*. Fili.

Horiya Hirashi, Horiya Atsushi. 1999. *Sonshi Goshi Zenyaku*. President.